APP NATION

Unleash the Power of Mobile Apps
to Supercharge Your Business
and Profits...even in a difficult economy

BRAD ADAMS

Cover image based on photo © Anton Balazh / Stockfresh

TABLE OF **CONTENTS**

ACKNOWLEDGMENTS

We would like to extend our thanks to several people for their assistance in developing this book. A very special thanks to Jeanniey Mullen of Zinio.com for insights and recommendations that contributed greatly to the discussion on these pages. Thanks also go to Chris Voss of The Chris Voss Show; Charles Warner, publisher of The Legacy Series Magazine; and Robert Yehling of Word Journeys, Inc.

CHAPTER ONE
WHY MOBILE APPS ARE THE FUTURE OF BUSINESS

When we celebrated New Year's Day 2009, few of us knew about apps. We may have heard the term, or figured it to be the abbreviated form of "applications." As in, "I just bought the new Microsoft Office for my computer. It's got some nice apps." Some, who knew what it really meant, might have downloaded primitive apps onto their "smartphones" — another term just beginning to seep into conversation. Everyone seemed to be preoccupied with the big tech-related buzzword making its way through society: texting.

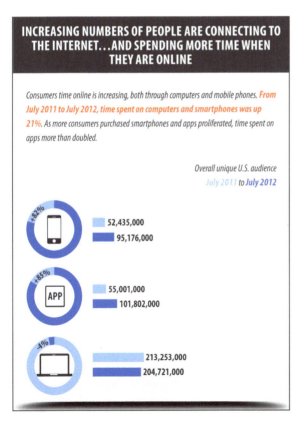

INCREASING NUMBERS OF PEOPLE ARE CONNECTING TO THE INTERNET...AND SPENDING MORE TIME WHEN THEY ARE ONLINE

Consumers time online is increasing, both through computers and mobile phones. *From July 2011 to July 2012, time spent on computers and smartphones was up 21%.* As more consumers purchased smartphones and apps proliferated, time spent on apps more than doubled.

Overall unique U.S. audience
July 2011 to July 2012

+82%
52,435,000
95,176,000

+85%
APP
55,001,000
101,802,000

-4%
213,253,000
204,721,000

How far we've come. It feels like we live in a different world than just a few years ago, doesn't it? All we hear about now, it seems, are smartphones, tablets and apps. The words are part and parcel of everyday conversation; often, they link together like a double compound word: "Smartphone-tablet-apps". Whether chatting with employees in our offices, shopping for gifts at the mall, or catching up on the day's news or football scores, most of us rely more and more on apps. It's like the new highway that cuts through your favorite forest; you might despise its existence, but you get to your destination faster, so you eventually use it. If we have teenaged kids around (or younger), we often find them downloading or talking about new apps like we used to discuss baseball cards, school dances, teen idols, or our favorite rock groups.

What are apps? For the sake of this discussion, the term refers to applications built specifically for tablets (such as the iPad, Asus Transformer Pad, Google Nexus 7 or others) and smartphones (such as the iPhone, Android, LG Optimus 2, Windows Phone or others). You might also come across the term "mobile apps". Mobile apps and apps are the same thing.

Thanks to the meteoric rise of tablet computers and smartphones with 3G and 4G connection speeds, apps are here to stay. They not only dominate the future course of business and society, but they define much of that course. Apps buy products, take surveys, make reservations, fill prescriptions, schedule appointments, promote discounts and sweepstakes, offer specials, notify us of product releases, remind us of upcoming events, give us news, track inventory, and broadcast the latest game scores. As of December 2012, there were more than 2 million readily available apps for all cell phone and tablet computer platforms. Thousands of public and private apps are being developed and added daily.

Whether you're a large corporation, or a small business with local or regional customers or clientele, your reality is the same. To proceed into the future without connecting to your target audience through specifically designed apps is to proceed at your own peril. The time will come, soon, when a business without a well-conceived, strategic app will be as disconnected as a portable typewriter in a computerized world.

"For any size business, the 'app' has become the Holy Grail of branding," says Jeanniey Mullen, executive vice president of Zinio, the world's largest distributor of digital magazine content. Zinio makes it possible for hundreds of magazines to distribute content digitally through their apps. "Previously, companies looking to build a brand through awareness, engagement, and loyalty had to invest in a multi-channel marketing effort that could often be costly.

"With the advent of mobile apps, a company brand can now be present with your consumer or prospect regardless of how close or far they are to your business," she adds.

The numbers back up Mullen's "Holy Grail" characterization. App use is the single fastest growing part of our technology experience. It's going to keep growing, too, especially when you consider the words of technology expert Mary Meeker: "We're in spring training here." According to Nielsen, from July 2011 to July 2012, the overall unique audience (different users) for mobile apps skyrocketed from 55 million to 102 million. That's just the beginning. The time spent monthly on mobile apps more than doubled, from 58.8 billion minutes in July 2011 to 129.4 billion in July 2012 — a 120% increase. That came after a 91 percent increase between 2010 and 2011! During the same time, increases in mobile web use (22 percent) and PC use (4 percent) paled by comparison.

Let's drill into the numbers a little further. In July 2011, the average mobile app user spent just over 1,000 minutes per month on those apps — just under

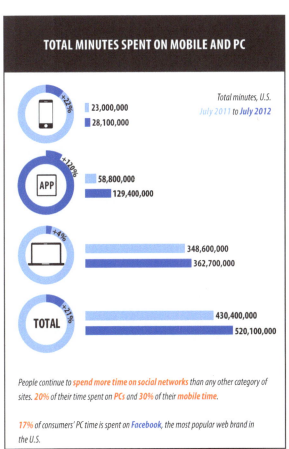

17 hours per month (approximately 35 minutes per day). In July 2012, the average monthly usage jumped to 1,268 minutes (42 minutes per day). The most committed users, which comprised 50 percent of this group, spent 98 minutes per day on their mobile apps. They spread that time across an average of 48 apps per smartphone customer. Not only are app users increasing in number, but also they're spending more time buying, selling, reading, and planning their lives on their smartphones or tablets. "Within two years, our smartphones will become our wallets," Mullen says.

How do apps travel? Through smartphones, tablet computers and some mobile phones. Before Apple launched the iPad in April 2010, the term "apps" was little known outside the application development and computer industry; now, it is a household word. According to one study, more than 15 billion apps have been downloaded since that first iPad launch. Smartphone and tablet ownership has skyrocketed in the past few years, and is quickly catching up to ownership of laptop and desktop computers:

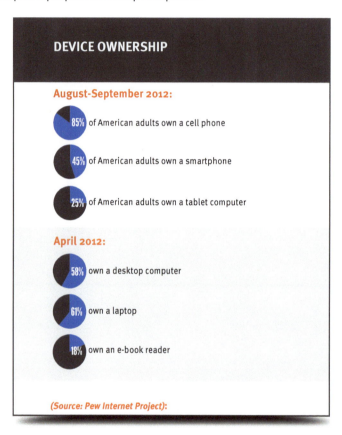

DEVICE OWNERSHIP

August-September 2012:

85% of American adults own a cell phone

45% of American adults own a smartphone

25% of American adults own a tablet computer

April 2012:

58% own a desktop computer

61% own a laptop

18% own an e-book reader

(Source: Pew Internet Project):

Now for the flip side. The biggest growth area for future app use comes from adults. Unless your business specifically caters and sells to teens and children, adults make the buying choices that create your revenue. The Pew Research Center's Internet & American Life Project showed that, in 2011, 40 percent of adults downloaded at least one app to their smartphones, and 75 percent downloaded to their tablets. Only 30 percent of the 2,260 adults in the survey used as many as 3 to 5 mobile apps per week; 60 percent of that group was what we could call frequent users, tapping into 6 to 10 apps each week. However, nearly half of the group said their main reason for downloading an app was to enhance their shopping experience or to make a purchase.

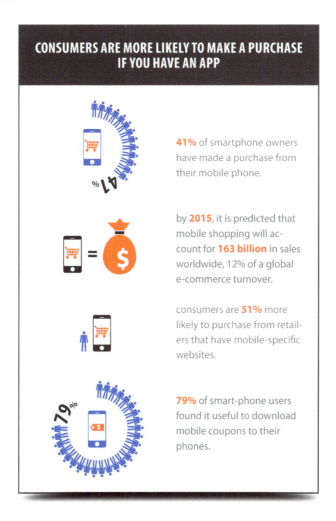

CONSUMERS ARE MORE LIKELY TO MAKE A PURCHASE IF YOU HAVE AN APP

41% of smartphone owners have made a purchase from their mobile phone.

by **2015**, it is predicted that mobile shopping will account for **163 billion** in sales worldwide, 12% of a global e-commerce turnover.

consumers are **51%** more likely to purchase from retailers that have mobile-specific websites.

79% of smart-phone users found it useful to download mobile coupons to their phones.

Those are the overall numbers. When you examine the mobile app question from a business standpoint, equally striking results pop up. Since 2010, more than 100,000 businesses created customized apps for their customers and services through just one of the more than 20 do-it-yourself app development centers now in the marketplace. According to a 2012 survey conducted by the Small Business and Entrepreneur Council, 31 percent of small businesses with 20 or fewer employees are utilizing mobile apps — up from 6 percent in 2010. The surveyed businesses cite gains in productivity, paper reduction, and the ability to meet rising consumer expectations for a more dynamic mobile experience. We will talk more about the consumer's powerful position in today's business world in Chapters Two and Nine.

One thing is certain: customers can no longer be considered silent "end users." They won't be silenced. They are vocal partners in the success of your business. If they don't buy, you don't succeed. They realize it. More and more want to conduct their business on apps. If you're still not sold, consider this projection by retail consulting firm Deloitte: The "mobile influence factor" (or effect of smartphones on in-store sales) on retail purchases will increase to $689 billion (or 19 percent of total store sales) by 2016. Much of that will be driven by customers checking out locations, specials, new products and in-store deals on retail apps.

That statistic alone points to why customer satisfaction should be first and foremost in your decision to produce an app for your business. The others, as suggested above, are increased productivity and decreased cost. According to the Small Business and Entrepreneur Council survey, small businesses are saving more than 725 million employee hours annually by using mobile apps. We will break down the reasons why as we move along. Suffice to say, payroll costs are a constant source of concern for small business owners. If you have the option to take action that will substantially reduce your payroll costs while enhancing your efficiency and productivity, do you exercise it?

THE GROWTH IN MOBILE SHOPPING

66% 66% of US smartphone owners use their phone to aid in shopping *(Source: Leo J. Shapiro and Associates, 2012)*

64% 64% of smartphone owners use mobile devices to shop online *(Source: eDigitalResearch and Portaltech Reply, 2012)*

34% 34% have made a purchase using their mobile phone compared, to 19 percent in 2011 *(Source: DC Financial Insights, 2012)*

25% 25% of smartphone owners say they have purchased something on their mobile devices in the past week, while 60 percent have purchased online and 87 percent in physical stores *(Source: Wave Collapse, 2012)*

25% 25% of consumers engage in online shopping only *Source: Prosper Mobile Insights, 2012*

Let's get back to customers. Every month, more adults take the plunge and buy apps. When they realize app usage is like riding a bike – second nature, once learned – they immediately seek ways that apps can make their lives easier. Just like Amazon.com and Netflix proved a decade ago with online shopping, adults will take the simplest, most efficient route to buy goods and services. Especially when excellent customer service is built into the online relationship. When asked why they download apps, half the surveyed adults cited shopping or making purchases. If the mobile app helps them think, shop, schedule or act locally, they will download it. Especially if it costs less than $20.

The bottom line? Small businesses with local or regional target market focuses tend to benefit more than other enterprises when they build apps to better serve their customers.

What a compelling big picture for mobile apps! And their significance increases with each passing day. Some of your competitors likely deploy apps to streamline their businesses and remain connected 24/7 with their customers; others use them to deepen and enrich the customer relationship. Quite simply, business is headed in a mobile direction, like the rest of our hooked-up society.

Chris Voss, one of Forbes Magazine's Top 50 Social Media Influencers, minces no words about it. "Mobile will be everything," Voss says. "Demand will be everything. All media, cable, news, music, TV, professional services, retail operations and everything else will be forced to submit to mobile demand. People will want everything accessible by their mobile devices. There will be huge disruption in these industries and serious revolutions of economy. It will also happen in other sectors as they become more technologically driven."

Voss is far from alone in his perception. Influential social media and business experts including Apple CEO Tim Cook, GE Senior Vice President Beth Comstock, Zinio's Jeanniey Mullen, and Mark Shapiro, president of the Consumer Electronics Association, make the same forecasts in different words. If businesses don't make regular mobile contact with their customers through apps, they will likely become next-generation casualties in much the way Wal-Mart left small town mom-and-pop stores in the dust.

If you haven't already done so, it's time to move into the world of apps. How do you get there? How do you determine which features are right for you? How do you make sure to build them to maximize your contact with customers, and to give those customers the timeliest information on your products and services? How do you make their lives easier and their loyalty to your brand or company stronger? How do your apps continue to evolve as your business grows and changes through their use?

That's what this book is about. In the coming chapters, we will walk inside the mind of today's hooked-up consumer. We will explore why smart businesses have fundamentally changed their relationships with their customers and clients. We will dive deeper into the services, options and features you can integrate into your app that gives your customer the greatest possible experience — and leaves you with the marketing data, cost savings, social media connection, and increased revenue you desire. Finally, we will review the ways to create the best, most customized app to build for your business.

It is a new world in the marketplace, one that often boils down to a tiny icon on a smartphone or tablet.

Let's step inside that world, get our feet wet, and see what all the fuss is about.

CLICKING IN: TAKEAWAY POINTS

- More of your current and future customers than ever use smartphones and tablet computers to fulfill their shopping, working, entertainment and communications needs — a number that will continue to increase
- The mobile app has become the Holy Grail of branding, the most direct contact you can have with a customer outside your place of business
- The 50 percent most committed mobile app users spend more than 1 ½ hours per day using their apps — and climbing
- Direct purchases made by smartphone have amounted to 13% of all U.S. retail sales in 2012 — triple the percentage from 2009.

CHAPTER TWO
POWERFUL AND CONNECTED: TODAY'S CUSTOMER

"The purpose of a business is to create a customer."

— Peter Drucker

A routine trip to the shopping mall reveals a world our parents and grandparents could only imagine. If they read a lot of Asimov, Bradbury, Burroughs and Heinlein, that is. Men, women, teens and older children walk with ear buds connected to music devices, their thumbs tapping furiously on smartphone keys. Or, they huddle together, watching the latest episode of their favorite TV show on hulu.com, YouTube video, a movie trailer on Yahoo!, or a streamed Netflix movie. Some race through mobile websites for movie times, even though the theater is all of 200 yards away. Others check sports scores while sifting through their shopping bags, or app-hop, bouncing from icon to icon to see which stores are offering the best specials. Big line at the checkout counter? No problem: we'll just tap the app, find what we want, select the right color, find the shopping cart, hit "send," and wait for the package to arrive overnight. And save 20 percent for shopping online.

When you observe customers today, it becomes easy to understand why corporations and businesses shell out billions of dollars a year to figure it out. Ten years ago, few businesses in any industry knew what "customer focus" was. They assumed it meant customer service. Now, corporations require their management teams, and even their rank-and-file workers, to understand and practice customer focus — the ever-changing habits, preferences and tendencies of the target market that, when realized, lead to efficient customer service.

You don't have to spend billions, millions or even thousands to know your target customer. You just need to know what motivates and interests them about your product or service. How will you connect with them to make the sale? In that sense, the mobile app has replaced the "three foot rule" known to salesmen: if someone is within three feet, you can shake their hand. And make a sale. Now, the app becomes your extended hand.

The quest to understand and please today's customer has led to some strange bedfellows, indeed. At electronics and audio tradeshows, the product engineers of Sennheiser, manufacturer of top-of-the-line headphones and audio equipment, talk directly with retailers and consumers. To appreciate that practice, imagine Ford compelling parts designers to help sell cars.

It doesn't happen that way...right?

Actually, it does. Today's business, health care, retail, professional services and fitness customers operate with decision-making clout never seen before. Because of the Internet, they can access information on products

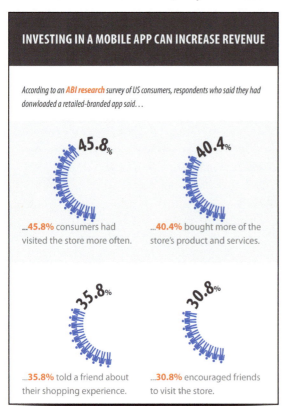

INVESTING IN A MOBILE APP CAN INCREASE REVENUE

*According to an **ABI research** survey of US consumers, respondents who said they had downwloaded a retailed-branded app said...*

45.8%
...**45.8%** consumers had visited the store more often.

40.4%
...**40.4%** bought more of the store's product and services.

35.8%
...**35.8%** told a friend about their shopping experience.

30.8%
...**30.8%** encouraged friends to visit the store.

and services instantly, and purchase without seeing or speaking to a live face. Since 2002, annual online sales have jumped from $52 billion to $256 billion, according to Statista. Half of those sales were retail. Another third were travel and flight-related. Wonder why the travel agent is going the way of the dodo bird? Not because of poor performance; good travel agents are masterful at customer service. Technology simply caught up, and replaced friendly faces with Expedia, Kayak, Priceline.com and airline websites. That alone is a cautionary tale of how far customers can, and will, go to find the best deals.

If your website doesn't provide the information customers seek, they will visit another website and you may lose the business. Likewise, if your website is tough to navigate and blanketed with material, they will move on rather than waste another second. If a customer finds something good (or bad), they may text, email or post their findings to their friends. If they contact you and do not get the answer they seek, or the help they need, they will move along to the next business — and let others know. Talk about viral word-of-mouth advertising!

Patience is not a virtue for today's customer. Nor are attention spans high. Many businesses have gained or lost revenue in a matter of moments because of what they posted or did not post on their websites. Furthermore, they helped or hurt themselves even more by the way they adjusted to what similar businesses in their localities or industries offered.

Most businesses today suffer from a lack of customers, a byproduct of technology and the sluggish economic recovery. Let's face it: the brick-and-mortar glory years of customers relying solely on you or your staff for information to make buying, patient, or client decisions are over. The dot-com boom of the late 1990s introduced consumers to a faster, easier way to learn what they needed to know. Remember when customers would spend their way through a few service professionals, site developers, suppliers or product lines to find what they wanted? Look in the rearview mirror. Those days are history. The Great Recession of 2008-2009 took care of that. What remains is an economy growing at a painfully slow pace, an underemployed work force in a society desperately trying to switch from the industrial to digital age, full-time positions without benefits, and no silver bullet in sight.

What does it mean? For starters, you have to work harder than ever to gain a customer, and then work even harder than that to motivate the customer to return for more. Today's customer typically buys less, is more price conscious, searches more for deals, goes online more, and is not as brand loyal as before. Everyone tries to save money. Everybody searches for a combination of great products and small sticker prices. That lesson re-enters our lives – and stores from coast to coast – every day after Thanksgiving, on Black Friday. It returns three days later, on Cyber Monday. According to Statistica, Black Friday 2012 generated $59 billion in sales. According to the Adobe Index, online consumers spent another $1.98 billion on Cyber Monday. Those were the top buying days of the year by far, both in stores and online. Many of those sales, both in-store and online, began from smartphones and mobile apps.

How do you deal with this sea change? How do you prosper when the customer is often smarter about the product than your part-time salespeople, knows exactly what he or she wants, and will move on if you don't have it — now? How do you make it work in a faceless business world of automated phone service, and call centers based in India?

Know your customer like never before. Provide greater customer service than ever.

The customer must be wowed by the information and quality of the product or service you provide. Then, he or she must be massaged and coddled with the perception of special treatment, coupons, or offers. If you want that customer to return, exhibit greater salesmanship and more creative marketing and promotion, not only in person, but online. Never has brand loyalty been tougher to maintain than today, when a teenage girl, for example, can pick up her smartphone, app-hop, and compare prices and styles between 20 shoe brands in less than 20 minutes.

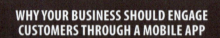

WHY YOUR BUSINESS SHOULD ENGAGE CUSTOMERS THROUGH A MOBILE APP

More than **33 million U.S. customers** already engage in shopping-related activities on their mobile phones.

2.3 million of those customers have made a purchase on their devices.

By 2015, **81%** of U.S. cell users will have smart phones.

What a handful. Yet, you *can* get ahead of the curve and become a magnet for new and returning customers. This can happen by taking a fresh approach to how you view customers:

1. Treat the customer as your business partner. Why? If they don't pay, you don't sell. They are just as important as a partner. They understand and utilize that feeling of empowerment very well.

2. If your customer has a complaint, let them vent. Listen without interrupting. Look for solutions within their comments.

3. When a customer suggests a new service, or a change to your approach, ask questions. Learn as much as you can to improve your service.

4. Follow through on the customer's input. Make improvements, or offer new products or refined services, that can benefit all customers.

5. Let customers know why you can or cannot do something. Be very honest and transparent. If you say you can do something, or provide a product, they will hold you to it. Under-promise and over-deliver.

6. Role play. If you're a retailer, ask a teenager to play a difficult customer (not hard). If you're a service provider, attorney or doctor, play the role of a reluctant client-patient who knows they need someone, but doesn't want to admit a legal or health issue.

7. Focus on what the customer needs, more so than what you want to provide them. What good is it to hard sell a family on a luxury Mercedes when they really want a "mommy van," an SUV? When roleplaying, focus on the takeaway — what information or service will best suit the customer. Then figure out how you will provide and convey that offer to the customer.

8. Make experience your greatest teacher. Evolve. Change approaches and technology to meet your customers where they stand. Be flexible and adaptable. Learn from every interaction.

9. Turn your customers into promoters. When you hook up to websites, e-mail marketing, social media and mobile apps, give your customers the tools to tell their friends about your great products or service — so they can tell their friends. Expand your target market and customer base by using the same communications tools.

Let's look deeper into this last point. Start by understanding how your customers use smartphones, tablets and the Internet. They research products and services, compare prices, seek input or opinions from their friends, and then decide whether or not to buy. If they want to buy, you need to have your sales hand extended. That is best served with an app.

Also, realize that a customer spends an average of five seconds on a website landing page before deciding his or her next action: to purchase, bookmark the page for a future visit, or move on. When they are accessing you through a smartphone or tablet, you also have five seconds to convince them.

Remember the first recommendation, to view your customer as a partner? That holds true for who they are, as well as what they want. Consider your customer to be just as receptive to new ideas, offers and ways of gaining maximum value from their purchases as you would be in their position. Come up with creative, innovative ways to gain their business. Think promotions, two-for-one offers, free consultations, discounts on prescriptions, or rewards to customers who make referrals. A doctor in Ramona, Calif., a semi-rural town east of San Diego, advises her patients to pick up their prescriptions at a particular pharmacy that charges 15 to 30 percent of what their competitors charge. In other words, a $20 prescription at the discount pharmacy runs from $65 to $125 elsewhere. She also discounts for office visits that turn out to be nothing more than minor check-ups. Not surprisingly, she has a booming business, with patients visiting from a 75-mile radius.

Understand how you can reach out to customers in the most immediate, direct manner. Meet them in the middle. Without customers, you have no revenue, and they want more convenience than ever. Make their experience with you memorable, something they will want to tell their friends, family, associates and colleagues about. When you do that, you will grow with your customers, and they will grow with you.

Today, this form of growth extends through their center of entertainment, commerce, communications and social interaction — their smartphone or tablet. That's where the mobile app comes in.

CLICKING IN: TAKEAWAY POINTS

- Your customers want instant results like never before. The average customer spends five seconds on a website page. If you do not provide immediate information and assistance, s/he will go elsewhere. By using apps, they can make that switch in a matter of seconds.

- You have to work harder than ever to gain a customer. Once that new customer walks through the door or shops with you, take all measures to build a relationship and earn their repeat business. That means meeting them where they like to shop.

- Treat your customer as your business partner. Listen to their input. Act on their suggestions if they improve your overall service. Be honest and transparent.

CHAPTER THREE
THE APP
SOLUTION

A prominent magazine and newspaper editor recently made an interesting decision. After four decades of living in the ink-filled world of the printed page, she migrated online. She bookmarked the websites of more than 100 domestic and international publications she read regularly. Then, in 2012, she took it a step further. She downloaded apps to all of the publications on her smartphone and tablet. It took about five hours to bring the media world to her fingertips, so she could stay even more caught up and make informed decisions.

Migration and "conversion" stories like this are popping up everywhere. As digital technology visionaries Chris Voss and Jeanniey Mullen said earlier, the smartphone and tablet will become the most important devices to keep track of our bustling, fast-paced lives. For millions, they already are. From scheduling to shopping, getting medical advice to buying concert tickets, your target market is relying more and more on their smartphones and tablets. A Wave Collapse survey noted that 25 percent of smartphone users bought something with their smartphone in the past week. That's a lot of people who are potentially one click away from your products or services.

Mobile apps give your customers instant access to information they want or need. As previously mentioned, the app is your extended hand that crosses the divide between you and a potential or current customer, shakes it, and says, "How can I be of service to you? What products do you need? How can I make you our newest satisfied customer? In what way can I fulfill your visit?"

Apps contain a wide variety of features: appointment scheduling features, news and information, sweepstakes, coupons, online surveys, subscription orders, product or event promotions, online sales, customer reviews, video, audio, seating reservation charts for restaurants or concerts, blogs, and so much more (more on this in Chapter Four). A well-conceived and well-built app focuses on the products, services or information that are not only useful to your target market, but also likely to bring them back for repeat visits.

As mentioned before, there are more than 2 million apps readily available, and countless more developed within businesses, or between large corporations and their suppliers. Every day, thousands of new apps enter the market through independent developers. Most of these apps serve some aspect of the commercial marketplace; virtually all businesses are represented in the apps already developed.

However, Mullen cautions against what she calls the "Field of Dreams" approach, the thinking that if you build an app, a sea of future customers will magically bypass the other 2 million apps and be drawn to it. "The if you build it, they will come myth is exactly that when it comes to apps – a myth," she said. "A well designed, engaging app, with a compelling reason for existence,

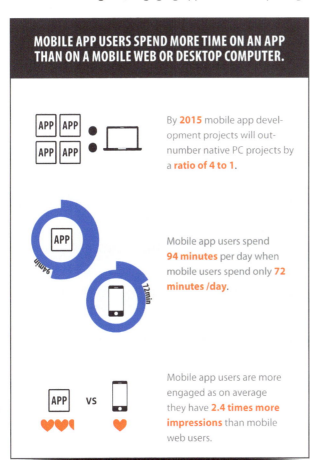

MOBILE APP USERS SPEND MORE TIME ON AN APP THAN ON A MOBILE WEB OR DESKTOP COMPUTER.

By **2015** mobile app development projects will outnumber native PC projects by a **ratio of 4 to 1**.

Mobile app users spend **94 minutes** per day when mobile users spend only **72 minutes /day**.

Mobile app users are more engaged as on average they have **2.4 times more impressions** than mobile web users.

can quickly create a place on the home screen of your most profitable customers. Today, over 90 percent of people who own a smartphone have it with them at all times. Your brand has never been closer to them. It's vital to have a presence, but quality is key. Invest in your app strategy, design and upkeep. Your app is not the place to cut corners."

Why has app use exploded? Why will they define a greater part of how business gets done? Let's look at a few ways of viewing and relating to customers in our wired world that we introduced in Chapter Two, from the perspective of app development:

1. **Treat the customer as your business partner.** If you produce an app that brings the very latest updates, developments or specials to your customer, that person will feel special. You will find yourself with a loyal partner-customer.

2. **If your customer has a complaint, let them vent.** If your target market is under 40, they will share ways to make your business better. Your app can register their concerns instantly.

3. **Follow through on the customer's input.** If a customer wants quicker service, or more responsiveness to their needs, you've got the perfect tool with your app.

4. **Let customers know why you can or cannot do something.** If they see something on your app, they know you can do it.

5. **Focus on what the customer needs, rather than on what you want to provide.** An app forces you to condense your overall business offering. You have to focus on what the customer needs, and where the greatest demand lies. It streamlines your business in a hurry. Streamline into the most revenue and content rich areas.

6. **Make experience your greatest teacher.** Apps can evolve along with your business. They should evolve and be adjusted to every significant change. They can be updated continuously. Experience not only becomes your teacher, but your ticket to sharper, smarter business.

7. **Turn your customers into promoters.** If your app, service or brand hits the mark with a customer, s/he will let people know about it in ways our predecessors could only dream about — virally, through social media, e-mails, texting and forwarding.

All of this sounds great — the customer service, the numbers. Still, how do you determine if you really *need* an app? If you've been selling construction equipment or plumbing supplies to the same steady clientele for 30 years, or providing legal services to a steady stream of private and corporate clients, you may not think you need one. If your restaurant traffic has always been steady, or the customers in your floral shop or athletic shoe store keep coming back, why bother? If word-of-mouth keeps landing you landscaping contracts, or your small real estate company sailed smoothly through the market of the past five years, why turn to anything else?

These are valid questions. No one wants to mess with proven success. How can you be sure new customers will find you if you invest in an app? How can you train yourself and your staff this new technology, after slugging through all the other new technology you've had to learn over the past 10, 20 or 30 years? Isn't training them in quality salesmanship and customer service enough? Isn't app development through-the-roof expensive, both to build and deploy? Not to mention the learning curve involved?

Again, all valid questions, except for one major caveat: Mobile app and web technology now feature a *low-cost point of entry*. Also, *deployment* has never been easier. Apps are so relatively low-cost, and easy to deploy, that they have become a business tool many companies will never again live without. Unless the next great innovation renders apps more and more irrelevant, as streaming music did with the CD.

Which brings us to another question: Can you afford to move forward *without* a mobile app?

We have already established that cost is not nearly the factor it was just two years ago. At that time, the average cost to develop an app was $10,000. Some apps ran as high as $100,000. Now, depending on the features you want, the interactivity of the app and whether you go with standard or custom features, the cost is a small fraction of those Pleistocene Era (2010) numbers. Like every other advance in information technology, once apps connected with their audience, found a market, and began to be downloaded by the thousands, then millions – and now, billions – the price to build them plummeted. This is discussed more comprehensively in Chapter Ten.

Next, consider if you want to have an app, or if you need one. We will explore this further in the next few chapters, so you can determine how essential it is to incorporate an app into your sales, marketing and promotion programs.

Once you've made this call, what kind of app do you need? There are basically two purposes for an app:

INTERNAL EMPLOYEE APP: You might use this to help your staff manage sales, produce invoices, monitor vendor transactions, or track inventory. Will the app simplify and make easier your employees' jobs, or complicate them? Will it increase productivity? Will it reduce overhead?

CUSTOMER-FACING APP: Will an app help your business better retain existing customers while drawing in new ones? Can it generate new revenue streams and opportunities? Does it help you keep up with, and/or surpass, your competitors? If you offer a product or service outside the norm, you can get a big jump in the marketplace by deploying an app.

One other consideration concerns how well you know your customers' use of smartphones. What percentage of your customers uses them? The vast majority of apps need smartphones or tablets, and the customer base of every business differs in percentage of use. About 50 percent of all cell phone users have smartphones (172 million subscriptions in the U.S. as of 2012), a number that will continue to rise in the coming years. For example, in a survey conducted by leading Internet research firm Kleiner, Perkins, Caulfield, Byers (KPCB), 33 percent of those asked said they wanted to buy an iPhone in the next six months. The respondents' age range? Six to 12. Furthermore, mobile web traffic as a percentage of total Internet traffic has more than tripled in the last two years, to 13 percent. When you consider that, on Black Friday, 24 percent of the $59 billion in total purchases were made online, it's safe to say many of your customers are also devout smartphone and Internet users.

You next consideration is to figure out how much development you need. Also, you need to decide whether:

1. You will invest the time to develop it yourself or with one of your IT people
2. Utilize a licensed development platform
3. Seek out device-specific app stores that provide partially built apps (typically, 50 to 75 percent development); or
4. Think as an innovator and create a customized app with a licensed platform *and* experts who consider your specific needs first

We'll review these options further in later chapters. Now, let's look more closely at the features and options that apps contain, and create a checklist to see which would be best for your business.

CLICKING IN: TAKEAWAY POINTS

- The mobile app is your extended hand when greeting a customer who shops with smartphones or tablet computers. Be sure you provide the vital information they need to make a buying decision or choice to work with your company.
- Just because you build a mobile app doesn't mean customers will magically appear. You must promote and market the app. Bear in mind that the best promotion of all, word-of-mouth, results from a smart, intuitive app that makes the life of your customer more efficient, as well as saving them (and you) money.
- App development prices are the most economical ever, and deployment has never been easier.
- Can you afford *not* to build an app?

CHAPTER FOUR
WHAT'S IN AN APP?

Imagine the spirit of the Wild West during its wildest days. Add the creativity of many of the land's sharpest technology developers. Mix them together, and you get a sense of the atmosphere in which mobile app developers ply their trade. The field is wide open with possibility and growth. Potential, as-yet-untapped features for future apps seem limitless, like a horizon that keeps extending. As Mary Meeker says, this is spring training for the app's run. Truly, the three biggest questions you need to ask, in order to focus your specific needs for an app, are:

- Does your app contain the features you need to serve your customers?
- Does it improve your market reach and bottom line?
- Does it assure ease-of-use for the customer?

If you randomly download 100 different "stock" and custom-built apps, and list all of their features, your list may extend beyond your office door. The beauty about apps is that practically any feature can be developed for a specific need. The better you define your needs, the more valuable your app will be. We'll get into this more thoroughly later. Also, apps are like websites: they can be changed easily and constantly, keeping them current and relevant for a public that thrives on both.

In this chapter, we will present and describe a checklist of the more basic features found in mobile apps – features you will want to strongly consider. These features utilize core elements of any business strategy: marketing, promotion, sales, communication, customer feedback, and product or service description. They also offer the ease-of-use might be the most critical feature, since customers will turn away from difficult-to-navigate apps, just like they shy away from more complex websites.)

All of the features shown here work on the Apple iOS (iPhone and iPad), Android, and HTML 5 platforms. Remember, once you develop an app and make it operational, you can update:

• GPS DIRECTIONS: Gives customers directions to your business, or outer offices, from anywhere in the world.

• ONE TOUCH CALLING: No need to save phone numbers or contacts; one-touch call connects directly with the phone's contact list.

• TELL-A-FRIEND FEATURE: Satisfied customers can help make your business offerings viral by using this feature to share with others over email, Facebook, Twitter and SMS. The app is the ultimate word-of-mouth tool.

• BUSINESS INFORMATION: Integrates the information that you want to promote to customers. Examples include shoe specials, top menu items, or featured services.

• POINTS OF INTEREST: If you're a realtor or tour coordinator, this allows pinpointing of points of interest on a map.

• EVENTS FEATURE: You can show a list of business events that would interest your customers. This is also great for event promoters, theaters or concert venues, book signings, artists and musicians, gallery shows and other special activities.

• CONTACT INFORMATION: Allows customers to connect and communicate with your business in a variety of ways, including phone, email, Facebook, Twitter and through your website.

• FAN/FOLLOWER WALL FEATURE: A great feature if you use Facebook

event or business pages, or you post regularly on Twitter or LinkedIn. Allow followers to offer their feedback on your business for other customers to see.

• PUSH NOTIFICATIONS: This content management system enables you to send emails to customers to announce promotions, openings, special events, product sales, awards or special industry designations you received, and much more. It is an ideal instant promotion tool.

• GPS COUPON FEATURE: You can create coupons that customers can only redeem by using the app to check in with your business. This creates a huge incentive for cost-conscious customers.

• FLEXIBLE COUNTER FEATURES: Conduct smartphone or tablet customer surveys and other list-oriented features, such as a list of which medical services a customer may need, drawing both customer interaction and feedback. This gives you valuable information on customer preferences and buying habits.

• HELP CENTER: Answer your customers' questions immediately by offering a help center feature, which enables them to ask a question.

• MOBILE ADS FEATURE: You can work with mobile advertisement designers, and then migrate the ads into the app. These are especially effective when offering specials, new products or services, promotions of videos you might produce, or long-standing items that you might advertise over the course of a season, or a year.

• NOTEPAD FEATURE: A great new way to take text notes without the need for paper or computer (The iPhone 4S and 5 notepad is a great example). Furthermore, you can email them to employees, suppliers or partners at any time.

• PODCAST INTEGRATION: Many businesses have capitalized on the value of podcasts, mini-radio programs you can create from your computer. This feature allows customers to integrate the podcasts directly into their smartphones, tablets or recent model iPods.

• QR COUPONS: You can create promotional QR coupons with this barcode feature, which customers would then scan with their smartphones to redeem with you.

• SOUNDCLOUD INTEGRATION: This integrates any audio file into smartphones or favorite listening devices of customers, allowing them to

listen on the go. Music instrument businesses, record labels, bands, radio programming producers and other audio-based businesses find this feature very helpful. Soundcloud also delivers radio programs and podcasts. Wouldn't it be nice for your customers to hear a scheduled show related to your business or products?

• VOICE RECORDER: The audio version of the notepad feature, you can record voice notes while driving to work, or sitting in a meeting or conference, and email to associates, colleagues, employees, or partners.

• WuFoo Integration: WuFoo works with basic business forms, such as appointment schedules, online orders, feedback documents, invoices, payment schedules, workshop and conference registration forms, contact forms, customer satisfaction surveys, and much more. WuFoo can also be customized and designed, within the app, to suit your specific form needs with your logo and company theme.

• YouTube Integration: Uses links to direct customers to your YouTube videos, and can be updated every time you post on YouTube.

• Blog Integration: You can integrate one or more blogs that you or your staff writes by integrating the RSS (Really Simple Syndication) feeds with this feature. If blogging is a primary form of communication and updating customers/readers, this feature is very valuable.

There are also several basic features that work with photographs that you or your customers provide. These features allow you to display visual impressions of your products, store, and how satisfied customers are using them. They amount to visual endorsements:

• Email Photo Feature: Customers can take a photo, or send an existing photo to your business. Imagine how valuable this would be for your new or featured products, main courses or special events that impress your customers!

• Flickr Feature: This feature presents photos in a streamlined gallery layout. It connects app users directly to your Flickr account, enabling them to see products, designs, visual arts creations, signage, live events, indoor atmosphere and other photographs that promote your business. If you own the type of business that relies on visual presentation for success — real

estate firm, plant nursery, home building, landscaping, art gallery, restaurant, jewelry store, etc. — you should open a Flickr or Picasa (below) account. These pages potentially reach every Internet user, and they save you the time, money and server space of posting and storing them on your site.

• Picasa Feature: Serves the same function as Flickr, only from the Picasa photo gallery website. (Note: if you work with a photo gallery, choose one other to simplify your customers' search and viewing experience. Don't water down your efforts by working with both.)

• NATIVE IMAGE GALLERY: You can display images pertaining to your business as they appear on your website. This differs from Flickr and Picasa in that the images come from your home website, rather than linking to your Flickr or Picasa accounts.

Social networking features belong in any discussion of app building. A majority of businesses now incorporate social media somewhere in their communications, marketing, sales or promotion plans. With an app, everything can be funneled into clients' or customers' smartphones and tablets, giving them one-click access to your posts, tweets and updates. It also gives you access to your customers' favorite social media sites. Most basic app features include:

FACEBOOK INTEGRATION
TWITTER INTEGRATION
LINKEDIN INTEGRATION
MYSPACE INTEGRATION

Since email marketing is central to any communications strategy, every multi-purpose business app will do well to include an email-integrating feature. An email integrator imports your contacts for the purposes of email campaigns, which can run off your smartphone or tablet. Most app development platforms include all, or a combination of, the following options — one or more of which likely matches your email platform:

MAILING LIST FEATURE: This feature is the app version of a website opt-in page, where customers can give you email contact information. If they see something on your website or through the app that appeals to them, they will tap in their email address on their smartphone.

EMAIL CAMPAIGN INTEGRATION
MYEMMA INTEGRATION
CONSTANT CONTACT INTEGRATION
GET RESPONSE INTEGRATION
ICONTACT INTEGRATION
MAIL CHIMP INTEGRATION

For restaurateurs, café and coffee house owners, and customers who dine out, you can create an app with these features:

• OPENTABLE INTEGRATION: This allows customers to make restaurant reservations from your smartphone or tablet. It also gives you strong back-end market research on how many diners are reserving online, through your app, or calling.

• TIP CALCULATOR: This app calculates tips on the spot. It is a very valuable app if you dine out often, take clients or colleagues to meals, or host special events that involve dining.

Finally, if you're a retailer or conduct online transactions, you will want to incorporate that service into an app. With customers now making 13 percent of all purchases with smartphones — and climbing — it's imperative to give them the option to buy from your app. This begins with a SHOPPING CART feature that allows you to add or sell items through either the PayPal or Google Check Out payment options.

Basic app development platforms can also integrate the following online stores and their offered products into a shopping cart feature:

SHOPIFY
MAGENTO
VOLUSION
BIGSHOP

When you develop an app, you will be able to mix and match these features. As enticing as it might be to pack an app with tons of features, it will serve

you far better to decide what features serve your customers best, so that they can interact more closely with you and make buying decisions. Don't fall into the trap of diluting your app with a bunch of features that work at cross-purposes, just so you can claim you have the most extensive app on the block. For example, with your email feature, choose the option that integrates directly with your computer email program. More will not appeal to your customers.

Sometimes, less is more when it comes to building apps.

To gain maximum benefit from your app, evaluate your business from an entirely different perspective, and then specific values to each app feature that you are considering. In the next four chapters, we discuss these strategies and options.

CLICKING IN: TAKEAWAY POINTS

- Apps can contain countless features – with more developed every day. They include shopping, email, text, video, opt-ins, social networking, GPS directions, couponing, links to product catalogues, and much more. Learn the various features that can be incorporated into a basic app.
- Determine which features will best give your customers the sales, promotional and communication tools they need to interact with your company or store.
- If you are a retailer, be sure to focus heavily on a shopping cart feature that makes your transactions seamless and easy for your customer.
- App features include back-end elements such as demographic studies of your customers, market research information, and trackers of how often they visit your app or your website, and how long they remain with you before clicking elsewhere.

CHAPTER FIVE
WHAT ARE YOUR OBJECTIVES?

During the 2012 holiday season, a customer walked into a popular San Diego County camera and photography supplies store. She talked to a salesperson for about 30 seconds, picked out the exact digital camera she wanted, purchased it, and walked out the door. As she stood outside the store, she snapped an iPhone photo of the camera, and texted it to her friends — who were looking for ideas for Christmas and Hanukkah presents.

Inside, the salesperson and manager smiled. What a perfect transaction! The customer comes in, makes an impulse buy, and leaves ... right?

Or did it only seem impulsive? Here is what happened. The customer wanted to buy her husband a digital camera. She scouted out models on a few different manufacturer websites, comparing not only price, but also zoom magnification, video and picture quality, ease-of-use, and download features. Then she visited the websites of camera stores countywide ... and found a downloadable app that belonged to the long-standing store. She downloaded the app, and saw the camera was available. Done.

The owner could have run his business without the app. This particular store has served customers for 50 years. Many of those customers won't think of buying their cameras and equipment from anywhere else. Yet, the owner was smart. He knew his objective was to retain long-standing customers and continually welcome new buyers. He also watched more and more people playing on their smartphones in his store. He switched his thinking, and built an app. He honored his objective and planted a big seed into the store's future.

Ready to make simple changes like this in order to hook up more closely to today's tech-savvy customer? Ready open your business to a world of potential customers ... literally?

For most companies (yours might be one), incorporating a mobile app into your sales, marketing and promotional flow will require adjustments to the way you conduct business. It will also require you to think differently. Your father and grandfather's philosophy of "develop customers and clients slowly" still works for some, but now, you're competing in a customer-centric world where instant gratification means a lot. Fortunately, your app is the perfect tool.

When you wanted to increase your customer base in the old days, before the digital era, you:

- Sent out information or ran an ad campaign
- Followed up with telephone sales calls or personal visits from your sales reps
- Trained your in-store sales staff on customer relations
- Answered every question with a smile, informing and selling new customers at the same time

Tried-and-true customer service still exists. However, more than ever, you'll find information and ad campaigns handled with websites and digital ads, telemarketing conducted by services (many overseas) or recorded messages, in-store sales staffs less trained than ever (some even exasperating you by saying, "Look it up on our website"), and personalized customer service replaced by faceless icons and prompts. No company exemplifies this more than Amazon.com, masters of the art of faceless customer relations and online sales. One of Amazon.com's in-house credos is, "We *don't* want to hear from the customers, unless it's a book or product review." Why? Any other call would be a complaint.

Without a doubt, the practice of building, keeping and expanding customer bases has changed greatly. Yet, the core principles of customer relations and sustained growth remain entrenched in the three goals most businesses look to achieve when designing apps:

1. FREQUENT AND CONTINUED ENGAGEMENT: You want customers to visit your app weekly, if not daily. Make it appealing for them to do so. This leads to repeat business and brand loyalty, 21st century style. It also creates awesome upselling opportunities, which we discuss in depth in Chapter Eight.
2. HIGH USER RATINGS: As Jeanniey Mullen points out, "Nothing speaks to the quality of your product like the ratings your app receives. Well-designed apps are conduits to 4- to 5-star ratings, which in turn create earned

media opportunities on top-ten lists, and social accolades." Imagine how this can expand your marketplace!

3. MONETIZATION: This comes in many forms – in-app purchase, booking reservations, setting a doctor's appointment, or pre-ordering part of your bill of materials from a landscape nursery or building supply store. Your app should always be one of your key drivers of revenue, or provide the information that brings people to your company or store with transactions or business relationships on their minds.

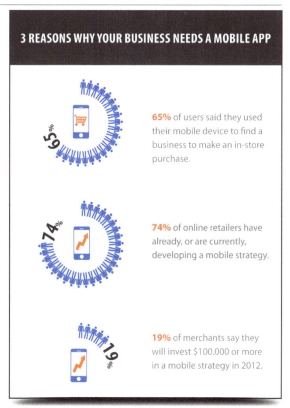

3 REASONS WHY YOUR BUSINESS NEEDS A MOBILE APP

65% of users said they used their mobile device to find a business to make an in-store purchase.

74% of online retailers have already, or are currently, developing a mobile strategy.

19% of merchants say they will invest $100.000 or more in a mobile strategy in 2012.

When you look at your business objectives in this manner, the road ahead becomes clearer and more familiar to your core practices, policies and principles. It also makes it easier to decide if you should work backwards from your overall goal of improving your process, or to begin a new process. Taking the three core objectives a further, we can ask:

1. How do we increase our number of customers in a way that reflects a personal touch, but appeals to the digital, wired world in which our target customers live?
2. How do we increase transaction value in a swift, creative way to customers that are accustomed to making quick decisions, surfing the web for deals, and transmitting their intentions instantly?
3. How do we keep customers coming back for more, over and over, when they are becoming less and less brand or business loyal on the whole?

Mobile apps enable you, to paraphrase a famous slogan, "reach out and touch" a lot more "someone's" than you ever could through store promotions or local ads alone. They also will help you fulfill your business objectives, once you clarify and sharpen them to include your app, website and/or mobile website program as a centerpiece of your sales, marketing and promotions effort.

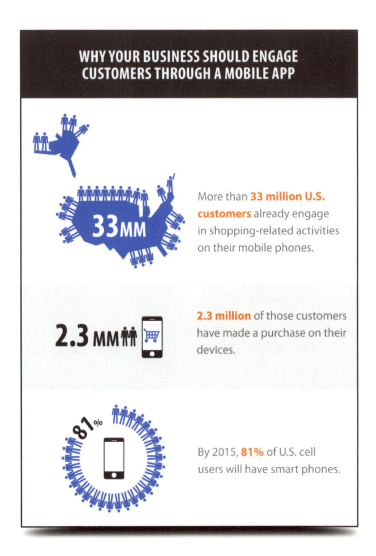

WHY YOUR BUSINESS SHOULD ENGAGE CUSTOMERS THROUGH A MOBILE APP

33MM — More than **33 million U.S. customers** already engage in shopping-related activities on their mobile phones.

2.3 MM — **2.3 million** of those customers have made a purchase on their devices.

81% — By 2015, **81%** of U.S. cell users will have smart phones.

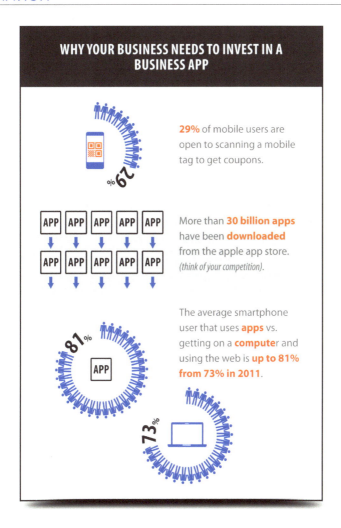

Like any other major business decision, developing an effective app, or a program involving an app, will require you to review your objectives. There are two ways to do this:

1. By working backwards from the goal you want to achieve, by determining the particular programs, products or services the app will best serve towards reaching the goal; or
2. Creating a new plan, and tying the app directly to it.

When reviewing objectives, most established businesses will find it easier to work backwards from the stated goal — whether it's 20 percent annual growth, a sell-out of the new product line, increasing restaurant reservations by 30 percent, or expanding the radius of your market by 50 percent. Newer enterprises, or businesses that have never done much online, will likely find it easier to start from scratch. In either case, the mobile app would serve as one of the key spokes of the sales and promotion wheel.

Some of the key questions that will help you determine your objectives for a mobile app might include:

• WHAT IS YOUR MOST COMPELLING NEED AS A BUSINESS FOR THE NEXT 12 MONTHS? Do you need more sales? Customers? A wider target market? Better promotion for products or services? An easier way for customers to connect with you? A way to crack into a younger market? Answering "yes" to any of these questions verifies that your objectives match well with mobile apps.

• ARE MOST, OR MANY, OF YOUR CUSTOMERS USING SMARTPHONES OR TABLETS TO CONNECT WITH THE MOBILE WEB? Know what devices your current customers are using; a simple print or online customer survey can determine this.

• HOW WILL YOUR APP MEET THE CUSTOMER SERVICE PRIORITIES AND OBJECTIVES THAT YOU CONVEY AS A BUSINESS?

• WHAT INFORMATION WILL YOU PUT ON THE APP THAT CAN BE CONSTANTLY CHANGED OR UPDATED? Make your information rich and "evergreen," so that customers keep coming back for more.

• WHO WILL YOUR MOBILE APP SERVE? YOUR CUSTOMERS? BUSINESS PARTNERS? EMPLOYEES? SALES FORCE? Customers and internal business apps are two different products; be clear about which you want your app to serve.

• IF YOU'RE A RETAILER, WHAT TYPE OF PAYMENT OR SHOPPING/INCENTIVE PLANS DO YOU WANT TO UTILIZE FOR ONLINE AND SMARTPHONE TRANSACTIONS? WHAT WORKS BEST FOR YOUR ACCOUNTING DEPARTMENT AND CASH FLOW?

• ARE YOU AN INFORMATION-ORIENTED BUSINESS? DO YOU HAVE AN INFORMATION-ORIENTED WEBSITE? If so, your business is a prime candidate for a mobile app.

• WHAT TYPES OF CUSTOMER OUTREACH PROGRAMS DO YOU WANT TO DEPLOY, BUT CANNOT, DUE TO LABOR COSTS? These programs might work perfectly through app deployment.

• DO YOU WANT TO INCREASE SOCIAL MEDIA USE TO ENHANCE YOUR BUSINESS PROFILE – AND MAKE IT EASIER FOR CUSTOMERS TO CONNECT TO YOU THROUGH SOCIAL MEDIA?

• WOULD YOU LIKE TO MAKE YOUR PRODUCTS OR SERVICES MORE AVAILABLE TO PEOPLE AROUND THE WORLD?

There are other questions to ask, but you get the idea. In order to determine how a mobile app can best serve you, ask questions that also address the features and best uses of an app. Once you become clear of your objective, choose from a menu of features, like those in Chapter Four, to help meet your objective.

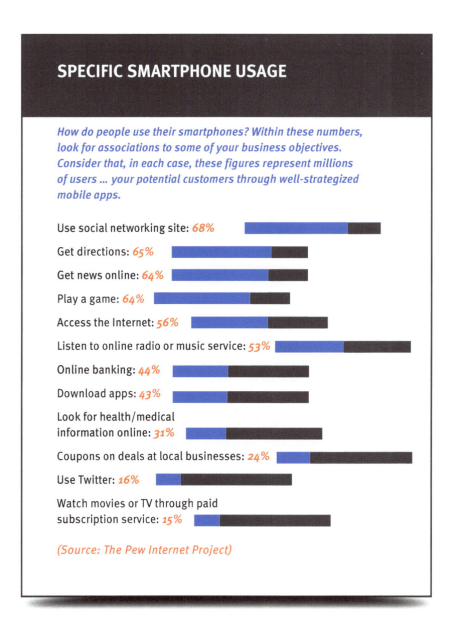

SPECIFIC SMARTPHONE USAGE

How do people use their smartphones? Within these numbers, look for associations to some of your business objectives. Consider that, in each case, these figures represent millions of users ... your potential customers through well-strategized mobile apps.

Use social networking site: *68%*

Get directions: *65%*

Get news online: *64%*

Play a game: *64%*

Access the Internet: *56%*

Listen to online radio or music service: *53%*

Online banking: *44%*

Download apps: *43%*

Look for health/medical information online: *31%*

Coupons on deals at local businesses: *24%*

Use Twitter: *16%*

Watch movies or TV through paid subscription service: *15%*

(Source: The Pew Internet Project)

Let's look at a few different types of businesses, what their objectives might be, and how they can benefit from mobile apps:

RESTAURANT OR CAFÉ

Mobile apps can benefit a restaurant in many ways. Customers can:

- MAKE RESERVATIONS
- CHECK IN TO SEE WHAT THE SPECIALS ARE
- GET DIRECTIONS
- PLACE TO-GO ORDERS AND PAY FOR THEM
- PAY FROM THE TABLE, WITHOUT NEEDING TO EXCHANGE CASH OR CHARGE CARDS
- SURVEY THE MENU — WHETHER AT HOME, ON THE ROAD, OR IN MEETINGS.

A mobile app greatly benefits more reluctant customers as well, who won't drive around to search for a good restaurant, or drop in without knowing of the establishment or being a regular customer. By downloading your mobile app, they can seek you out in a much more comfortable way.

Now look at what you, the restaurateur, can do at your end:

- UTILIZE YOUR MAILING LIST (WHICH YOU OBTAINED FROM CUSTOMER SURVEY CARDS) TO SEND PUSH E-MAIL MESSAGES TO YOUR CUSTOMERS' SMARTPHONES
- THANK THEM FOR VISITING
- NOTIFY THEM ABOUT SPECIALS
- OFFER PREMIUM SEATING OR SPECIALS FOR RETURN VISITS
- ANNOUNCE UPCOMING EVENTS
- SPREAD THE NEWS ABOUT NEW CHEFS OR ENTREES
- SEND A "PERSONALIZED" MESSAGE TO CUSTOMERS WHO HAVEN'T DINED WITH YOU IN AWHILE
- INSTALL GPS COUPONS TO REWARD FREQUENT BUYERS

FITNESS CENTER

Fitness centers split their customer focus into two areas: providing quality workouts and workout facilities; and creating and promoting repeat visits and long-term.

Let's look at both. A fitness center can use a mobile app to focus its service side — quality workouts and facilities — in these ways:

- ANNOUNCE NEW EQUIPMENT OR TRAINERS, AND THEIR CREDENTIALS
- ANNOUNCE NEW FITNESS PROGRAMS
- POST CALENDARS OF CLASSES AND PROGRAMS BY THE WEEK OR MONTH – AND PUSHING THEM TO REGULAR CUSTOMERS VIA EMAIL
- MOTIVATIONAL QUOTE OF THE DAY, FROM AN ATHLETE OR FITNESS EXPERT
- WORKOUT SCHEDULES FOR CUSTOMERS BEING TRAINED BY EMPLOYEE-TRAINERS. THESE CAN BE ADJUSTED REGULARLY.
- PROPER USE OF SPECIFIC EQUIPMENT — "THE STATION OF THE WEEK"
- DIET AND NUTRITIONAL ADVICE
- STRETCHES OR YOGA POSTURES OF THE DAY OR WEEK

For the sales and marketing side, a mobile app would provide:

- REGISTRATION OPTIONS AND OPPORTUNITY FOR CUSTOMERS TO PAY ONLINE
- MONTHLY PAYMENT PLAN ONLINE
- GPS COUPONING FOR DISCOUNTS OR REFERRAL SPECIALS – "SIGN UP A FRIEND, GET ONE FREE MONTH"
- REVIEW OF THEIR PLAN
- SCHEDULING FEATURE
- FORUM FOR ASKING QUESTIONS/RECEIVING ANSWERS BEFORE OR AFTER A WORKOUT
- LOCATIONS AND DIRECTIONS

RETAIL STORES

If ever the mobile app were tailor-made for a specific type of business, retailing would be it. In the past three years, retail industry has experienced a 300 percent increase in online sales by smartphone and tablet. It's quickly getting to the point that retailers who do not deploy mobile apps are hurting their bottom lines substantially.

Here are a few advantages mobile apps offer retailers:

- EASE OF SALE. A CUSTOMER CAN VIEW THE MERCHANDISE, DECIDE TO BUY IT, AND PAY THROUGH A SHOPPING CART
- COUPONING. YOU CAN PUSH COUPONS ON A MONTHLY, WEEKLY OR DAILY BASIS — FOR GENERAL DISCOUNTS, FOR PREFERRED CUSTOMER DISCOUNTS, FOR SEASONAL SALES ... THE POSSIBILITIES ARE LIMITED ONLY BY YOUR IMAGINATION

- REWARDS FOR LARGE PURCHASES OR FREQUENT CUSTOMERS. WHEN A LARGE PURCHASE IS MADE, OR A CUSTOMER CLICKS IN FOR THE 10TH, 20TH OR 50TH TIME, YOU CAN PUSH A SPECIAL COUPON OR FREEBIE AFTER THE SALE IS COMPLETE
- ANNOUNCE NEW PRODUCT LINES OR OTHER MERCHANDISE
- CUSTOMER SURVEYS
- FOR CLOTHING STORES, APP-BASED OPTIONS ON STYLES, COLORS, OUTFIT MATCHES
- LINKS TO BRAND NAMES CARRIED IN THE STORE, SO MOBILE CUSTOMERS CAN QUICKLY CHECK THEIR SITES FOR INFORMATION THAT SELLS THEM – AND THEN PURCHASE THROUGH YOUR APP. EVERYONE WINS!
- MAJOR STORE NEWS

CONSTRUCTION/ROOFING/PAINTING/PLUMBING/ LANDSCAPING COMPANIES

At first glance, construction and related industries don't seem to be good matches for mobile apps. However, consider these features and advantages you could deploy:

- INTERACT WITH CUSTOMERS OR VENDORS ON BILL OF MATERIALS, SUPPLIES, PLANT OR PRODUCT CHOICES WHEN CHANGES NEED TO BE MADE ON THE SPOT
- MOBILE ESTIMATING AND BIDDING, FROM ANYWHERE IN THE WORLD
- WORK OUT BUDGETS OVER THE SMARTPHONE OR TABLET
- HIRE AVAILABLE WORKERS FOR SPOT JOBS ON AN AS-NEEDED BASIS — FROM THE SITE
- CHANGING SCHEDULES ON THE FLY WITH YOUR VENDORS AND/OR EMPLOYEES
- LOCATIONS AND DIRECTIONS• INVOICING AND TRACKING HOURS
- CONNECTING WITH AFFILIATE COMPANIES, COLLEAGUES OR ADVISORS, AND SENDING PHOTOS TO WORK OUT A PARTICULAR CHALLENGE ON THE SITE

MEDICAL, HEALTH PROFESSIONAL OR LEGAL OFFICES

Doctors, healthcare professionals and attorneys have plied their trades on a combination of new and ongoing patients/clients for decades. Yet, more and more are building mobile apps for their practices because apps offer the greater ease of convenience to:

- REVIEW CASES WHILE OUT OF THE OFFICE
- INSTANTLY SCHEDULE, OR CHANGE APPOINTMENTS, FOR CLIENT/PATIENTS

- Schedule changes for surgery or court appearances
- Collaborate with other professionals on a specific case — and send a text, video or audio file to further study the matter
- Request prescriptions or refills, and get them filled before patients arrive at a pharmacy
- Locations and directions
- Reminders about appointments, procedures, filings or court appearances
- Answer questions or make adjustments to billing
- For attorneys, contact witnesses or experts without disrupting court proceedings – or the rest of their daily schedules, if nearby

In all of these fields, and so many more, specific uses for a mobile app go on and on. The key is to figure out your objectives, build those uses into the app, and become proficient. Also, if you are a long-time businessman and train younger members of your staff to serve as your online specialist(s), you will operate at an increased efficiency and see your bottom line fall as your profits rise. Remember: people under 25 grew up in this digital world.

"Really, your apps come down to just a few simple things," Mullen says. "First, there's simplicity/intuitive interface. If you have to provide directions on how to use your app, it is too hard. Second, make sure you have suggestive, entertaining user flow. Your app should guide your user through to the desired action without them realizing they were guided. They should enjoy their experience. And third, create hidden benefits. The most successful apps have hidden benefits, whether it is unlocking extra features, or offering exclusive access to something. Extra benefits for loyal users are a must."

As Mullen's comments suggest, it is very important not to be overly restrictive as you convert your objectives into mobile app strategy. It is also important to know two particularly efficient uses of the app, which we will discuss next:

- Mobile advertisements and coupons about your products, services or specials; and
- Social networking

CLICKING IN: TAKEAWAY POINTS

- What are your business objectives? What do you offer a customer? What does the customer expect from you? How do you see your company growing forward? Answer all of these questions clearly before moving further with your preparation to create an app. The more focused your objectives, the more effective your app.

- The practice of acquiring, keeping and expanding your customer base has changed as customers migrate online. However, the three core principles remain the same, whether helping an in-store customer or designing an app: frequent and continued engagement; high user ratings (customer satisfaction); and ways of making revenue.

- As you prepare to build your app, ask yourself: Who will this app serve? A business-to-business app is completely different than an app that serves consumers.

CHAPTER SIX
MOBILE ADVERTISING

One of the biggest decisions any business owner makes is to determine how much money to allocate for advertising. A question follows: "What type of advertising will connect me with my current and future customers?"

Advertising comes in many shapes and sizes. In the pre-Internet era, a small business would run campaigns around newspaper, newspaper circular, magazine, the Yellow Pages, billboard, radio and/or local television ads. Other opportunities might come from newsletters, handbills and flyers distributed at major public events or fairs, accessory items (such as logos and addresses on pens or calendars), or even people standing on street corners wearing signs (realtors and tax accountants come to mind). Special advertising periods for retailers would include post-Thanksgiving (for Christmas), after-Christmas, Easter, Summer, and Back-to-School.

Fast forward to 2013. We may as well be living on a different planet. Advertising has made a quantum shift to the digital world, both driving and following media itself. Now, on any given day, you will see ads on your favorite online newspapers and magazines, advertising choices on hulu.com's Internet TV feed, image or text ads on social media and search sites like Facebook, Google and Yahoo!, ads on Internet radio and large-circulation blog sites, and ads pushed by e-mail marketing campaigns.

Some traditional channels for advertising still remain. However, print newspapers are well on the road to extinction, and print magazines are heading to digitization if not there already. The recent decision of Newsweek to discontinue its print edition after 80 years and switch to an

Image Courtesy of DirectTV

entirely online format bears this out. Newspapers and magazines are the two biggest print media casualties of the digital age. Radio and television commercials remain strong, but continue to lose dollar and market share to their Internet counterparts. Billboards will remain viable as long as we drive on roads and highways, but the other niche advertising forms are falling by the wayside. Have you noticed how thin Yellow Pages directories have become? Or that 20 *million* businesses now advertise through the online Yellow Pages?

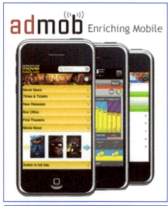

Image Courtesy of AdMob

If a national advertiser wants to push a display ad campaign, it can do so through print and digital newspapers and magazines, an Internet banner ad, a social media ad, pop-ups on tablets and mobile devices, and Google and Facebook ads. That's just text and photos. Imagine how wide that universe becomes when you add voice-overs, audio, video, direct consumer participation and other features of the 2013 Advertising Universe.

Whether your target market is local, regional or national, you face far different advertising choices than previous business owners. In fact, if you're over 40, you might feel like Alice after she fell down the rabbit hole. It's not enough for you to grow accustomed to e-books, digital magazines, podcasts, texting, mobile websites, streaming radio, social networking and TV. Now, you need to learn more about how these forms of media best promote your message to customers who live with and through their devices.

That's where mobile advertising comes in. It is one of the fastest growing forms of advertising in both the business-to-business (B2B) and business-to-consumer (B2C) worlds. Mobile advertising connects your brand's message and image to your target market through tablet computers, smartphone or other mobile devices; cellphones, Kindle Fires and recent-issue iPods can receive mobile ads as well. In 2011, mobile ad buys totaled $1.6 billion out of $30 billion spent on total Internet advertising. Consider the number to be like Apple or Amazon.com stock in the late 1990s; you will never see it that low again. Mobile ad provider Millennial Media predicts that, in 2017, mobile ad revenues will climb to $6.6 billion.

Businesses that have utilized mobile ads since the "early days" — say, 2012 —

are moving into a new phase. Top mobile ad agencies report that some businesses are developing strategies specifically connected to mobile ads. They build their strategy, and then make their media buys. This is a 180-degree flip from the early adopter stage. Remember when the Internet was new, and many companies rolled out sexy features, bells and whistles, before realizing that content, functionality and performance carried the day? We've hit that cusp in the mobile ad business now. Which is great news for you.

MOBILE ADVERTISING: BY THE NUMBERS

30 Billion - Total spent on Internet-based advertising in 2011

1.6 Billion - Total spent on mobile ads in 2011

74 - Percentage of smartphone users who have not received a mobile ad from their favorite brands

68 - Percentage of men likely to make purchases via mobile ads

64 - Percentage of smartphone users who have made a smartphone purchase after seeing a mobile ad

58 - Percentage of women likely to make purchases via mobile ads

(Source: 2012 Mobile Advertising Survey, Millennial Media, KPCB)

If your customer base is under 40, or if you are marketing toward that age group, you may miss the boat if you don't run mobile ads. This applies even if your entire target market lives within a 10-mile radius of the main office. One example: According to xAd and Telemetrics, mobile searches for restaurants listed on website directories or running mobile ads result in a *90 percent visit*, order or reservation business conversion rate — *64 percent within an hour*. Likewise, more than half of the people who find dining coupons on their mobile devices will visit that specific restaurant.

So what is "mobile advertising"? What types of ads fall under this title? On what devices do they move? A quick introduction:

High-End Mobile Ads

High-end mobile ads run on smartphones, which support Internet browsers that can display websites similar to those on a desktop or laptop computer.

The zoom features of smartphones make it easier to navigate pages.

There are two types of high-end mobile ads: text ads and image ads. Text ads look like ads on a desktop computer. However, you don't have as much room on a smartphone screen, so you need to choose fewer ads per page. The emphasis is on creating more impactful ads. Remember the landing page rule, that you have five seconds to sell the customer? It definitely applies with

Image Courtesy of Chevrolet

mobile text ads.

Image ads are exactly that — pictures that sell your product, service or event. While they can be as large as a desktop screen on a computer, you are greatly limited on size on a smartphone. Most mobile text ad designers suggest you go with 320 x 50 pixel banner ads (approximately 3 inches by ½ inch).

WAP Mobile Ads

Wireless Access Protocol (WAP) mobile ads enable users to browse mobile websites, which are specifically designed for mobile devices. Think of mobile websites as miniaturized versions of the parent website.

As with high-end mobile ads, WAP ads appear as text or image ads. However, there are notable differences to their high-end counterparts. Text ads give up to two lines of text, with 12 to 18 characters per line, depending on the language. The third line contains your website address; you can use either a hotlink to the site, or a "Call" link to allow customers to call you.

Do you need to build a mobile website for people to view your mobile ads? Not necessarily. Customers can call or email directly — or visit your main website — if you add the appropriate link to your ad. However, mobile websites are ideal for customers who want to see what you offer but not access an entire website from a smartphone or cell phone.

You can house all of this advertising activity through your mobile app. It is the fastest, most convenient way for people to interact with your business, make purchases or place orders or reservations while on the go. In other words, they can see your mobile ad and respond to it immediately. How's that for bang for your buck?

Here are a few specific areas in which connecting your mobile app to your advertising campaign can draw in new customers while growing relationships with existing customers:

PRINT AND TEXT ADS: Mobile print and text ads are enjoying higher conversion rates, especially in the retail, content sales, ticket sales, and dining industries. If it's product-oriented or consumable, then a mobile ad is well worth deploying from your app — or by pointing your app to a mobile website. Be sure to make your ads catchy, specific and sparse with text. Use as few words as possible. Remember that you can link to your website, mobile website, or outside reviews to give the customer more. They can find more information if they want it. Mobile ads can be built at a low cost (your mobile app developer can handle it directly or point you in the right direction). They can also be changed rapidly, and gauged for effectiveness by the number of visits or clicks they receive.

MOBILE COUPONS: Mobile coupons are becoming among the stickiest ways to reach out and touch that customer — and save them money while making a sale. Coupons trigger quick buying decisions. During Black Friday 2012, numerous retailers stuck coupons into position as the first feature that shoppers saw when clicking the retailers' apps. You can do the same for any product or service.

Surprisingly, men are more likely to utilize mobile coupons than women, while the opposite is true for print coupons. Perhaps it is because mobile coupons pop up in real-time, when it takes a more immediate, impulsive decision to hit "Buy." And we all know how most men will do anything to get in and out of stores quickly! According to the Mobile Advertising Survey, 35 percent of men will redeem mobile coupons, compared with 27 percent of women. If you push a mobile coupon, and 200 sufficiently wired customers see it, you stand a chance to make approximately 60 sales. That's effective advertising.

How important are coupons? According to the Mercator Advisory Group,

55 percent of consumers are interested in receiving mobile coupons, but only 10 percent have actually received one from a merchant. If you're looking for an edge in market share, and a way to target more customers and keep them coming back, coupons offer a distinct approach and advantage for you.

MOBILE ADS AND TV: A new term is buzzing through the entertainment, media and publishing worlds: trans media. It means different things to different businesses; it's a 21st century version of "multimedia". When speaking of mobile devices, apps and ads, a dynamic example of trans media would be to combine TV viewing with smartphone and tablet browsing, while running a similar message or similar content across all three platforms.

If you already buy local television ads, or infomercials, and then tie in mobile ads, you can create the Perfect Customer Storm — in a good way. Here is what happens when a customer watches TV, simultaneously browses their devices, and your TV ad pops up:

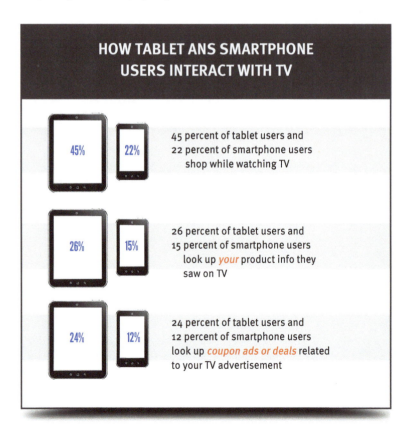

See the writing on the wall? If you synchronize a TV ad buy schedule with coupon ads, and make them available through your mobile app, you will create a rich, dynamic buying experience. It is the online version of a perfectly merchandised store window that begs customers to walk inside and buy what they see.

Mobile ads are getting the job done for more and more businesses. When you partner them with your overall mobile app development, you make it even easier for touch customers. That's always the goal.

CLICKING IN: TAKEAWAY POINTS

- Mobile and web-based advertising, along with Facebook and Google ads, are replacing newspaper and magazine advertising as the preferred "ground game" for industrial, commercial, white-collar and retail advertising.
- Mobile advertising sales will quadruple in number from 2012 to 2016. Consequently, more businesses than ever are mapping their advertising strategies around mobile devices and apps, rather than considering them a minor add-on to already existing campaigns.
- The relationship between television advertising and programming, smartphones and tablet computers continues to tighten. An increasing number of mobile users respond quickly to advertising they see on TV.
- Apps move mobile ads and mobile coupons across smartphones and tablets. Mobile coupons are becoming very popular among retailers.

CHAPTER SEVEN
WORKING WITH
SOCIAL NETWORKING

For all of the talk about iPods, smartphones, tablets and the other dramatic technological developments of the past decade, nothing has swept through global communications like social networking. Anytime something connects fully one-quarter of the world's population, we tend to take notice. As we figure out how utilizing social networking creates great advantages for our businesses, we realize the incredible power that lies at our fingertips.

The relationship between social networking and business has become a torrid romance. Social networking provides an Internet-based connection between one person and another, a connection often deeper and more personal than face-to-face meetings (good for long-distance business, bad for personal interaction). Countless people have reacquainted with old friends, business associates, or high school buddies. Relationships have kindled or re-kindled. New business has been created. Discoveries have been made. You can use posts, tweets, updates, chat rooms, forums, bulletin boards, freelance services, photos, audio, and video to announce or present almost everything concerning personal lives or business. You feed this into your social network, which potentially reaches out to touch the entire world beyond it. It's like launching a satellite into space: you intend for the signal to benefit people on Earth, but who else might be listening in the universe?

Posts and updates also have the potential to "go viral" — to connect with your fans, friends and followers so deeply that those people post it to their networks, which spread the word to *their* networks. If you remember high school and college algebra or calculus classes, you know where this goes — exponential growth. Those 1,000 people you informed about your hot new product just created a potential marketplace 10, 100 or even 1,000 times that large by reposting or retweeting your news. When you give your customer the added capability of socially networking with you while on the move, through your mobile app, you empower your business that much more.

Many businesses still fight over the question of whether or not to social network. The more pressing question is this: *how can they afford not to?*

Frankly, a business that does not utilize social networking runs a major disadvantage in today's marketplace. It's like putting a 135-pound person into an NFL backfield. Social networking drives people to your website, allows you message in a real-time way to customers, vendors, partners or associates online, and helps you promote products to a potential world of customers. When you utilize it well, you create communities of satisfied customers who chat with each other (and their friends) about your products or services, and much more. Social networks literally extend your business. There are countless ways to use them, a few of which we'll dive into later.

How big is social networking today? The following statistics from research firms Nielsen and NM Incite bear out the numbers of people in the United States (total population: 308.7 million, according to the 2010 Census) who frequent the Top 10 social networks.

MOST POPULUS SOCIAL NETWORKS

Facebook:	152.2	million
Blogger:	58.5	million
Twitter:	37	million
Wordpress:	30.9	million
LinkedIn:	28.1	million
Pinterest:	27.2	million
Google+:	26.2	million
Tumblr:	25.6	million
MySpace:	19.7	million
Wikia:	12.6	million

(Source: Nielsen and NM Incite)

While LinkedIn is best identified with business use among the names on this list, all 10 are used for both business and personal purposes. Also, note that not every site on here is a quick posting site. For instance, Blogger and Wordpress are primarily blogging sites, Pinterest is a behemoth among online bulletin boards,

MySpace caters mainly to the music industry these days, and Google+ has grown out of Google's search engine and email features.

As Zinio's Jeanniey Mullen notes, you possess tremendous latitude for how you work with these social networks, and how these networks operate in concert with each other. "Checking through Google Maps, Foursquare and Facebook makes a ton of sense. Recently, I was on my smartphone, looking up the location of a local business on Google, and found that if I checked into that location once I got there, I would get 15 percent off. This achieved a few things: I went to the location; I checked in and saved 15 percent; and now, I go back all of the time because I know I can always check in. And then I told many friends about this 'secret' I unlocked."

There you have the full spectrum, in one person's experience: social networking between platform and business, using a smartphone and an app, finding an incentive to do business, and spreading the word to friends.

That illustrates the first set of numbers. Now, let's look at some of these sites and their unique audiences through mobile apps and the mobile web:

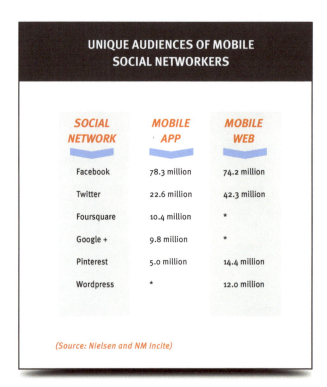

UNIQUE AUDIENCES OF MOBILE SOCIAL NETWORKERS

SOCIAL NETWORK	MOBILE APP	MOBILE WEB
Facebook	78.3 million	74.2 million
Twitter	22.6 million	42.3 million
Foursquare	10.4 million	*
Google +	9.8 million	*
Pinterest	5.0 million	14.4 million
Wordpress	*	12.0 million

(Source: Nielsen and NM Incite)

Notice the tremendous increase of social network volume moving through smartphones and tablets? This story really gets interesting when you compare the year-to-year increase in overall social networking subscriptions to the increase through mobile apps and mobile web:

SOCIAL NETWORK INCREASES, PC vs. MOBILE DEVICES (FROM JULY 2011 TO JULY 2012)

NETWORK	PC	MOBILE APP	MOBILE WEB
Facebook	-4%	+88%	+85%
Twitter	+13%	+134%	+140%
Blogger	-3%	n/a	+100%
Pinterest	+1,047%	+1,698%	+4,225%
Google +	+80%	+86%	n/a
LinkedIn	0%	n/a	+114%

(Source: Nielsen and NM Incite)

Telling, isn't it? In five of the six social networks featured in this table, usage increases on mobile apps and mobile web far exceeded their PC counterparts. Consumers and businesses alike are not only calling, texting and shooting photos on their smartphones, but also conducting their social networking on there as well.

Now, we will move into the "stickiness" of these sites — how well they grab and hold onto visitors. Also, let us look at how long your current and potential customers spend socially networking. What you will find, in looking at the following infographic, is just how captive your current and potential customers are once they enter the social networking world:

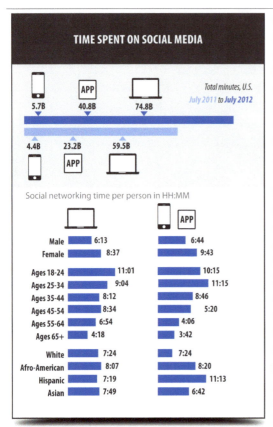

Let's look at these numbers from a business customer standpoint. According to Nielsen and NM Incite, consumers spend 30 percent of their time online visiting social networks through mobile devices, and 20 percent through PCs. That reverses the numbers from 2011. In addition, total time spent on social networks jumped 37 percent during the past year, up to 121 billion minutes in July 2012. Now for the kicker: consumer time spent using social media on either mobile apps or the mobile web accounted for 63 PERCENT of year-over-year growth. When you consider mobile app use grew by 85 percent and mobile audience as a whole climbed 82 percent, while PC use only edged up 4 percent, you see what keeps your marketplace up at night — and busy during the day.

When you look within the strategies of the social networks, a sea change is happening to accommodate this mobile migration. Mobile apps tap into existing social networks to create added connectivity and community-building features for businesses and consumers alike. Meanwhile, web-based social networks (Facebook, Twitter, LinkedIn, etc.) are utilizing mobile features and accessibility to drive even more features and information options to their users. This change occurred while mobile web evolved to allow full mobile access to the Internet.

Since they have different platforms and properties, the social networks work differently between smartphones, tablets and websites. For instance, it is easy to send a Facebook post from either a tablet or smartphone, or a Twitter tweet. Blogger involves writing article-length content, so it is not ideal to create on a smartphone, but tablets are tailor-made for the job. Conversely, Google+ is an excellent network for on-the-go people who direct their communications through their smartphones.

The other growing trend in social media and social networking concerns advertising. All of the social networks that carry advertising report increases in the numbers of ads being sold, as well as gross impressions (number of people who see the ads). However, and most importantly for you as you connect with core customers and increase customer base and revenue, there is also a jump in advertising pass-along between network-connected friends. A Nielsen survey showed that 26 percent of social networkers are more likely to pay attention to an ad posted by one of their Facebook friends or people they follow on Twitter. Another 17 percent feel more connected to brands or businesses seen on social networking websites. Furthermore, 26 percent of consumers are OK with ads popping up based on their profile information or personal preferences, like you see before TV shows begin on hulu.com.

These percentages are very significant. They demonstrate how the tried-and-true "word-of-mouth" practice between friends has merged with the viral world of social networking. The numbers also suggest that your catchy ad, or well-branded message, can play right into the customer's sense of camaraderie he or she derives from social networking. If a consumer likes your Facebook ad, Google ad or a mobile ad you break across their social network, they might well tell their acquaintances in a post or tweet. If someone has 5,000 Facebook friends or 25,000 Twitter followers ... it paints an enticing picture.

How can you promote and market your products and services through social networking? Here are just a few of numerous strategies and options:

- GENERAL INFORMATION ABOUT NEW PRODUCTS OR SERVICES
- SHOW AN ITEM FROM YOUR PHYSICAL OR ONLINE STONE, AND LINK THEM TO THE LARGER DISPLAY OF PRODUCTS ON YOUR WEBSITE
- PROMOTE SPECIAL OFFERS OR DISCOUNTS
- ANNOUNCE SPECIAL EVENTS, PROMOTIONS
- OFFER FREE PDFS ABOUT YOUR SERVICES, LINK TO YOUR SITE, AND INVITE (OR REQUIRE) THEM TO LEAVE BEHIND THEIR E-MAIL ADDRESS WHEN THEY DOWNLOAD THE PDF
- COUPONING AND TARGETED ADVERTISING
- NEWS POSTS ON VISITORS, SALES, NEW PRODUCTS OR SERVICES, OR OTHER ITEMS OF INTEREST TO YOUR CUSTOMERS

- DE-FACTO CONSULTING, SHOWING LINKS TO ARTICLES OR STUDIES ON AREAS RELATED TO YOUR BUSINESS
- POSTING YOUR NEWSLETTER AS A PDF OR LINK – AND GIVING IT A CHANCE TO GO VIRAL AND DRAW IN MANY MORE SUBSCRIBERS, AND FUTURE CUSTOMERS

All of this is great, you say, but what does it have to do with developing or not developing a mobile app? All mobile app developers offer basic social networking features — including Facebook, Twitter and LinkedIn — that you can build into your specific app. When you do, countless possibilities lie at your fingertips. Take Twitter, for example. "It is very simple to integrate a twitter feed into your app," Mullen says. "This feed can call local or national tags into a conversation. If your content is speaking about the best yoga class in zip code 12345, your app can pull in a feed to see what others in that zip code are talking about, or, better yet, what people who are talking about yoga find important. It is a very low cost way to make your app very engaging."

As we discussed in Chapter 4, app development platforms also offer an email tool specifically matching your email program and database. Put the two together, and you create a powerful way to reach both your current customers and target market. If you include an email opt-in for visitors who click onto your app, they might sign up and then tell all their friends on Facebook what they just did. Or, if you are a systems or marketing consultant, they might Tweet about their experience and aim followers to your website or mobile website.

When you tie social networking to your business, you vastly expand your potential market. You also give customers a forum for talking directly with your company or about your company. Potential customers who previously knew nothing about your products or services are far more likely to learn of you through their social networks than by randomly searching the Internet and finding your site. When you build social networking access into your mobile app, you make it even more personal, reaching out to meet those customers at their smartphones and tablets.

CLICKING IN: TAKEAWAY POINTS

- Businesses of all types and sizes harness a great advantage over their competitors by building a strong social networking presence. Why? That is where their customers spend many minutes or hours every day.

- Social networking offers the greatest word-of-mouth advertising potential in the history of business and commerce. A customer's or client's positive or negative experience with your business can be seen by thousands or millions of others within minutes.

- There are numerous ways to promote and market your services and products through social networks. Make it very easy to connect your customers to those pages, posts, ads and feeds — no matter which device they are using.

- Many key social networking options exist when developing your app. Be sure to incorporate the social networks with which you work through your website and advertising. Give your mobile app users the chance to interact with you.

CHAPTER EIGHT
UPSELLING: YOUR APP'S
LASTING VALUE

Barnes & Noble didn't win the bookstore wars solely because of its hundreds of locations, favorable wholesale pricing from publishers, or financial might. Those factors helped, but just 30 years ago, Barnes & Noble consisted of a few stores located in trendy Manhattan neighborhoods.

Image courtesy of BN.com

If not for money, storefronts and price breaks from pressured publishers, how did Barnes & Noble get from there to here, taking out B. Dalton, Waldenbooks, Borders, and every other chain seller along the way except Books A Million?

They mastered upselling. Barnes & Noble refined the art of creating repurchasing opportunities for their customers. They made people feel wanted and heard. When you walk into a B&N store, a variety of discounts on new arrivals, bestsellers, specialty items, seasonal items and clearance titles await you. You might find additional specials on specific genres or books by the same author, signing appearances, storytelling hours with kids, gift cards, and the Barnes & Noble membership card, which gets you 10% off anything in the store — and other savings throughout the year. This upselling strategy continues with the sales clerks, who ask for your membership card (or whether you want to buy or renew a card), and always suggest an add-on item at the counter — a bookmark, gift wrap, CD, DVD, magazine or calendar. The more astute sales clerks even tie their add-on questions to materials related to the authors of the books you're buying.

Smart, smart, smart.

That's the ground game. Barnes & Noble has also engineered an aggressive online upselling campaign. If you sign up to BN.com, you will receive weekly emails on the latest events, promotions or discounts across the chain — or online. For example, during the 2012 Christmas season, BN.com pushed out emails that offered:

* 50 PERCENT ONE-DAY DISCOUNTS ON ALL CHRISTMAS-RELATED BOOK TITLES IN THE ONLINE STORE
* 5 PERCENT OFF PURCHASES OF $19.95 AND MORE WHEN USING MASTERCARD
* 30 PERCENT OFF HOLIDAY COLLECTION OF TOYS, GAMES AND STUFFED ANIMALS (STORE ONLY)
* FREE TOY OR GAME WHEN YOU PURCHASE TWO AT REGULAR PRICE (ONLINE ONLY)
* 50 PERCENT OFF SECOND BOOK WHEN YOU BUY ONE BOOK AT REGULAR PRICE, PLUS THE 10 PERCENT BARNES & NOBLE MEMBERSHIP CARD DISCOUNT
* 50 PERCENT OFF LARGE-FORMAT, COFFEE TABLE BOOKS (IN SOME CASES, SAVING $50 PER BOOK)
* 50 PERCENT OFF THE SECOND NOOK TITLE WHEN DOWNLOADING THE FIRST AT AN ALREADY DISCOUNTED PRICE
* FREE GIFT WRAPPING IN SOME STORES (IN ONE, A GROUP FROM A DEAF SCHOOL WRAPPED BEAUTIFULLY, AND GRATEFUL CUSTOMERS DROPPED TIPS INTO A BASKET)

Anchoring every pushed email were the same three icons — Facebook, Twitter, and Google +. If you liked the email, Barnes & Noble invited you to pass it along, and view through their social media postings.

This is a large, creative upselling campaign. It illustrates how smart upselling enables a company of any size to continue drawing in their core customers despite the constant pressure from competitors (in this case, Amazon.com). With each customer visit, they strengthen the brand. Furthermore, all of these upsells can be viewed from Barnes & Noble's mobile app, and the online elements can be purchased from smartphones and tablets.

Attracting new customers is always the first goal of your business. Keeping them buying is the second. Without repeat customers, you cannot build relationships, receive word-of-mouth referrals (the best kind), or grow your business. You will always be at square one. When you upsell, you entice customers to repurchase from your store, theater, service, practice or firm. That builds loyalty to your business, to the *brand* that is your business.

We're loyal at heart; we don't like to switch gears too often. Why do you think many of us still use household, cleaning or personal hygiene products made by the same manufacturers we knew in childhood or young adulthood? Those manufacturers upsold our parents, and us, until we felt so comfortable and sure with their products (and the stores that sold them) that we would not want to turn anywhere else. Quick question: what percentage of people who used Apple computers in the early years has never used another brand? The answer: over 95 percent.

That's what every business wants. You want to leverage your hard work, fine products, top-of-the-line service and the efforts of your employees by making it easier to make money. Repeat customers do that. So do mobile apps. An app is today's perfect upselling tool. It accommodates a mobile society using mobile devices. The app increases repurchase frequency, enhances customer satisfaction with your products or services, and builds brand loyalty. Its combination of look-ins to your website or mobile website, social media options, email features, GPS couponing, and checkout/sales tool gives you the ability to offer additional or more expensive items, upgrades or other add-ons. Afterward, customers can tell their friends about it — and guide them to your app.

That's upselling, pure and simple. It's also upselling with the added benefit of word-of-mouth advertising. Combines these features, and you will soar right past your competition and flourish. You will create a path to prosperity during any economic phase.

How important is upselling? It keeps your doors open. Various business surveys show that up to 80 percent of both sales and long-term profit come from existing customers through upselling or cross-selling (for example, taking a woman who wants to buy a dress into the shoe or purse departments as well). It is far easier to re-sell an existing customer than to gain a new customer.

Let's look at a few upselling strategies, and how you can utilize mobile app technology to take advantage of them:

1. COMPLIMENTARY PRODUCT: "Buy one, get one free." "With your purchase of $20 or more, we will give you a free _____." "Free car wash with $100 gas purchase for truckers." Everyone loves a freebie. This simple strategy makes the customer happy, and often entices them to buy an add-on item. You can create these offers on your mobile app with coupons, push emails, or links to specific products on your site.

2. BUYING LARGER/MORE EXPENSIVE SIZES: You can use mobile apps to upgrade your customers' buying choices by offering option menus. For instance, if someone visits your gardening supply site looking for pruning shears, feature the more expensive model, and downplay the lower-ticket items. When presented with that option, many customers will buy up to own a higher quality product. They'll also appreciate buying it from their smartphone while busy with another activity.

3. CUSTOMER SURVEYS: Upsell through surveys. Ask your regular customers to complete an online survey accessible through your mobile app. Give them a discount toward their next purchase for participating. That shows how much you value their input, and gives them incentive to visit your location or app again.

4. TIERED SERVICES: Mobile apps work great for tiered services. If you are a car detailer, for example, you might offer four different levels of service, ranging in price from $39.95 to $79.95, or higher. Label those tiers: i.e. silver ($39.95), gold ($49.95), platinum ($59.95), titanium ($79.95). Use your website, or other advertising, to drive customers to the mobile app. Offer a 10 percent discount if they reserve through the app. Offer a break on their next detailing appointment if they upgrade from the level they would ordinarily choose. This upsell technique works well with apps for any type of tiered service, membership program or multiple product offering (such as gift packages).

5. AFFILIATING WITH OTHER VENDORS: Let's say you sell new or modular homes. You will make the sale in person, even though the customer might view your website. However, you can use your mobile app to create upsales by affiliating with kitchen, flooring or bathroom suppliers. The customer clicks into their offerings through your mobile app, uses the promotional code you provide, and gets 10 percent off their purchases. In addition to that, the kitchen, flooring or bathroom supplier gives you a 15 percent commission for affiliating with them. This works great in large-money sales that involve more than one vendor.

6. POP-UPS ON-SITE: This great upsell technique works between a mobile

app and your website or mobile site. Let's say you're an auto parts dealer. A customer planning a full tune-up pulls out their smartphone, clicks your app and finds the plugs, points and distributor cap they need. They purchase. After they give you the credit card information, add a pop-up before they hit "Buy." In the pop-up, offer a free PDF e-book on a "proper tune-up," and a $15 discount if they buy another item before leaving. Many customers will be so happy to receive the complimentary e-book that they will take you up on the discount.

7. DOWN SELLING: Sometimes, good upselling comes from down selling. Your mobile app is an excellent resource. Coupons, free add-ons for shopping on your app, and sharp discounts for a second purchased item (buy one, get the other 75 percent off) increase traffic. Down selling appeals to mobile app users.

8. CROSS SELLING. Mobile apps also work well for cross selling. Say you own a men's fine clothing store, and need to boost sales. When someone wants to buy a suit, what does a good salesman do? Leads them into the shirts, ties, shoes, socks and belt. When a customer clicks on your app and finds the suit they like, you can guide them to matching shirts, ties and accessories. Offer a 10 percent to 20 percent discount for those add-on items. It works.

9. EXTEND WARRANTIES THROUGH YOUR APP. When a regular customer's warranty on a product (tires, an appliance or lawnmower, for example) runs out, offer to extend it through your app. Offer a 10 percent discount. On a multi-year extension, offer an extra year for 25 percent or more off that year, again if they extend online through your app.

10. SELLING OPTIONS AND FEATURES. This strategy serves car dealerships and luxury item retailers especially well. When someone is shopping your site to purchase, allow them to use your mobile app to easily navigate the features and options available to them. They can make an appointment through the app, or even purchase some of the options for the car you have already sold to them. When they arrive to pick up their car, present it to them: with options already included. Use your app to make your customers feel well nurtured.

11. DELIVERY OPTIONS. Do your customers want their purchases quickly? Entice them to receive their goods immediately, offer that feature on your shopping cart, and watch them bump up their delivery service — and charge — through your app. Businesses can make 50 to 80 percent profit on delivery options, but you must couple your offer with sleek efficiency from your shipping team.

12. UPGRADED SERVICES. If you provide writing, communications or public relations services, own a legal firm, or are a health services professional,

you can upsell through richer services. For instance, you can offer a second press release at half the price of the first, or offer a menu on your website that provides opportunities to upgrade a brochure design. In all of these businesses, people are on the move and time is of the essence, so be sure your mobile app provides these capabilities.

Here are a few cautionary pointers when upselling through your mobile app:

1. PREDETERMINE THE BEST ITEMS AND TIMES TO UPSELL. Don't try a random, shotgun approach, or the same promotions over and over again. Strategize the items you want to feature. Be especially mindful of key buying seasons.

2. TEST DIFFERENT APPROACHES. An upselling strategy for an automotive parts store may not work for your yoga studio. Create approaches unique to your customers' needs, and rigorously measure the results to determine what works best. If you don't see a measurable sales, traffic or client increase, switch your approach. This is an ongoing process. The most successful, long-lasting businesses change their approaches many times. You can make these changes to your app as well.

3. DO NOT ANNOY THE CUSTOMER. Present your upsells as opportunities for the customer, or client, to receive more from you. If they decide not to buy, give them easy ways out of the transaction. A good model is Amazon.com, which offers three chances to cancel a transaction while taking customers from the online store to final checkout. Any lack of convenience will annoy the customer.

4. PROVIDE GOOD SUGGESTIONS. Post a strong Frequently Asked Questions section reachable through your mobile app. Describe your products or services explicitly. Offer add-ons that work: A corkscrew or bottle cover for the wine, a discount on notary services for signing up for other legal services.

5. PLAY ON EMOTIONS — AND COMMON SENSE. The easiest way to sell is by appealing to the customer's emotions. However, an impulsive buyer will become an angry buyer if the quality of your product or strength of your service doesn't match their expectations. Upsell with an eye for what enriches the customer's experience, not for your profit alone. Use common sense in the way you navigate them through your app.

There are many other upselling strategies. The sky is the limit: If you can come up with a unique, distinctive upselling idea that works with your product or service line, and can be promoted and delivered through your website, then your mobile app will give you a big frontline advantage.

The key to upselling is to leverage what you already have. Whether you can repackage features when you sell cars, convert your years of business consultation or legal representation into online courses or legal services websites, repurpose product information into online product stories or testimonials, or turn last year's clothing lines into this year's great add-on specials, use your mobile app to promote your intellectual as well as physical assets.

When you create an app that combines text, content, visuals, video and resources you already use in other channels, you can reflect and enhance the customer's experience with your physical business and website. When you promote an upsell, they will feel so comfortable and noticed that they will use your app to purchase more quickly — or from any location.

Consequently, you will enjoy greater customer satisfaction. You will also enjoy continuing profits through your greatest revenue stream — returning customers.

CLICKING IN: TAKEAWAY POINTS

- The mobile app is the best technological tool for upselling ever developed. It keeps your customer directly in touch with you every day. Never has your customer or client been so close to you on a 24/7 basis.
- Upselling keeps your doors open. Twenty percent of your customers buy 80 percent of your products and services. Use your app to continually deliver options for the loyal customer to do more business with you.
- All traditional retail and business-to-business upselling strategies can be adapted to the mobile app.
- When you develop upselling strategies that are specifically delivered through your mobile app, you create a major advantage over your competitors who are not connected to their customers through mobile devices.

CHAPTER NINE
DEEPENING YOUR CUSTOMER'S EXPERIENCE

A funny thing happened on the technology-created Road to Disconnect from personalized service: customers wanted to keep their relationships intact and personal with their favorite businesses and stores. While many business owners used technology to cut overhead, streamline operations, reduce labor costs and improve out-the-door efficiency, customers:

- GREW WEARY OF CALLING AND GETTING VOICE MESSAGES, OVERSEAS CALL CENTERS, OR THE SEEMINGLY ENDLESS LOOP OF MENUS AND OPTIONS
- BECAME FRUSTRATED WITH FACELESS VOICES, AND GENERIC RESPONSES TO THEIR QUESTIONS
- DECIDED THAT YEARS OF LOYALTY TO THEIR FAVORITE LABELS, BRANDS, ATTORNEYS, OR MATERIAL SUPPLIERS MEANT NOTHING IF THE SERVICE DIDN'T CONTINUE TO BE GOOD
- CONTINUED TO CRAVE WHAT WE ALL WANT — THE PERSONAL TOUCH

For 20 years, many businesses fended off these customer concerns as they continued to depersonalize the way they did business. They decreed that technology solved everything, and the customer had to adapt ... or else.

That ship has sailed. The truth of today's business world is very clear: thanks to the Internet, wireless technology, smartphones and tablets, the customer rules the roost. Businesses who don't realize that will sink faster than a hundred-pound rock tied to an anchor. The greatest story in global commerce in the past decade has been the consumers' noisy revolution. They recognized the power the Internet gave them to make buying decisions, switch brands or labels, and demanded quality service and product from many businesses that used to dictate what people would wear, buy, grow or build.

Now, everyone is preaching customer service. Corporations spend millions training leaders and managers. Smart businesses look for employees who are both socially refined and well versed on the company's policies, products, services, and marketing strategy. Customer surveys and focus groups have become today's hottest marketing tools, because we need to know what our potential customers are thinking, how they're trending, what motivates them to buy, and how these decisions will impact their lives.

Much of this intense focus on customer service is playing out online, where the customer controls the interaction. If this seems a bit far-fetched, think again: At any given moment, a customer is one click away from switching to your competitor. They no longer need to find new stores, theatres, parts suppliers or medical practices in other cities, or be held in the store until your salesmanship prevails. They can point — and click. That's power.

Nothing in the technology realm gives the customer more immediate decision-making power, or you greater positioning in our mobile society, than arming your marketplace with a mobile app hell-bent on assuring quality customer service.

Why mobile apps? Because they provide what customers have always wanted in their business dealings — fast service and a feeling of importance. Isn't this stating the obvious? Maybe, but apparently, knowledge has not translated into practice. Customers have never felt less important than during the past 20 years, when technology replaced human contact with voice mail, email, menus and options, robotics, and websites.

Consequently, customers have seized back the wheel of the ship. Now, they *will* form a relationship with your company, products and services. They *will* receive good customer service. They *will* find exactly what they need, at a price that fits their budget, and (for retail products), with shipping and delivery timing that meets their needs. If they ask questions, they *will* receive answers at the touch of a fingertip, zipped to them at 3G or 4G speed.

If not, they will point — click — move on. They will tell their friends about it through Facebook, Twitter, texting, a phone call, or in person.

This leaves you, the business owner, with two options: You can plow forward with business as usual, hoping your old model can ride out the storm of customer empowerment (spoiler alert: this particular tempest, like the eye of Jupiter, will never spend itself). Or, you can meet the customer in the middle and show them a dynamic way into your common future, by deepening their experience.

Websites can provide pages of description, detail and depth, a store and shopping cart, as well as good interaction and portaling to other sites or social networks. Mobile websites provide an on-the-go version. However, the days of constructing bloated networks and maximizing customer time on-screen to funnel through a pile of banner ads is over. For many smartphone and tablet users, that experience now feels like being sucked into a black hole. Fully half the U.S. population has switched its communications and information center to the smartphone and tablet.

This is where mobile apps save the day. They deepen customer experience by providing the richness of a relationship with your business at their beckoned call. They also exist for the smartphone-tablet environment, the new communications and information hub. Customers will use the app weekly or daily. It will become meaningful to their lives. It will serve a specific need at a specific time … every time they want to view your latest offerings or conduct business with you. Stay one step ahead of them, utilize their feedback, and make each experience more enjoyable than the last.

That's customer service today: viewing your customer or client as a *partner*, a person with whom you want to be in *relationship*. This holds true whether you're dealing business-to-business or business-to-consumer. By creating and nurturing a relationship that fulfills and makes their life easier, you will motivate your customer to contribute to the success and reputation of your business. This also goes for situations when your app may not be as responsive as you'd like.

Making your customer feel served means everything. No matter what, be honest and transparent. "Customer service is the most often forgotten element of the app," Zinio's Jeanniey Mullen says. "But it's the most important. Keep in mind that customers expect a great experience, and immediate access to support if they can't receive it. In the app world, many times issues are not related to your app, but to the device they are using. Customers don't care. Be responsive, proactive and most of all, over communicate in the cases where your app has an issue (and, it will have an issue at some point.) Customers respect responsiveness and sincerity."

Step into your customer's shoes, and imagine how their *experience* with your business feels. An experience is far more than a phone call, product demo, consultation, taking an order, trying on a few garments, answering a question or making a sale. That's *your* experience. The customer typically wants an exchange that combines friendliness, dialogue, knowing the stories behind certain products or services, learning something about your background (especially if you are engaging in a legal, medical, counseling or consultative transaction), inserting their two cents about what you offer, and working *with* you to decide which products/services will help them most today, and in the long haul. That's an experience, rather than a cold hard sell. The more you can see your business from the customers' point of view, the more success you will enjoy in today's customer-centric world.

What are some of the specific ways in which you can deepen your customers' experience through mobile apps?

- CREATE SPECIAL OFFERS AND COUPONS: Thanks to mobile apps, businesses can provide coupons in real-time. Talk about customer service! A great example is Rutter's, a convenience store chain in Pennsylvania, which created a mobile app so customers can get instant alerts about special promotions and deals available inside their stores. The app also gives them points for purchases, which earns them discount on gasoline. There are apps available that allow merchants to load offers, coupons and incentives into their own apps.

- LOYALTY PROGRAMS. Because of its intuitive qualities, a well-designed app can track customer purchases and visits, enabling you to offer rewards and benefits for long-term customers. In their physical form, these cards are limited by whether or not you can get to the store. Within an app, you can be anywhere to buy. You can create a mobile loyalty card, customize its look, provide defined tiers (e.g. gold, silver, bronze), offer personalized messaging, and promote add-on purchases based on customers' interests. Furthermore, you can study consumer trends through their app activity, content they shared with others, and where they clicked after finishing with you — or to spread the word about your loyalty program. If you give the customer an incentive-based buying program (and loyalty cards are that), and a means to spread the word, you will create many loyal *and* new customers.

- GETTING CUSTOMERS INTO THE STORE. Let's face it: if you have a store, or a physical location, you want people to walk through the door. Use your app to assist and motivate customers to visit your store by delivering text or rich media messages to offer specific sales at specific locations on specific dates.

- IN-STORE PRODUCT AVAILABILITY. You can make it much easier for your customers to find a specific product by offering categorized lists of your products through your app. That way, the customer can search the category and determine if you have the product, which beats the alternative — skipping over you entirely.

- **REAL-TIME PRODUCT REVIEWS AND COMPARISONS.** Promote the quality of your products and services by giving customers access to reviews through your app. Make the best reviews accessible with the app so that customers get a quick — and positive — impression. Customers who see positive product reviews will buy, and they will appreciate seeing the information in advance.

- **CUSTOMER SELF-SERVICE.** If you have a shopping cart, make it easy to navigate through your app. Emphasize ease-of-use in all of your interactions, but none more so than here. Ease-of-use is mandatory on a smartphone or tablet, because the customer is not visiting your office or store. Assure them of a rich, fast, enjoyable experience.

- **POINT OF PURCHASE SPECIALS.** Two things often happen when people visit a store: they can't find a product; or they play with their smartphones while waiting in line. Capitalize on these experiences. Make sure that your app focuses on the main products in your store, so that customers can quickly look up information and find the product. That may help to sell them. When they stand in a long line, be sure your app points to some point-of-purchase add-on items, so if they tap your app, they can find another item they may want to buy. Remember the old three-foot salesman's rule? When a customer is in your store, give them a reason to buy.

- **INCORPORATE QR CODES.** QR codes (the small squares that look like mazes and can be scanned by smartphones with the QR app installed) lead customers to deep links in your app. They bridge the digital and print worlds, and are becoming as common as bar codes. If your local business has a sign with a QR code for your business, or vice versa, this allows you to compliment your online and offline strategies. Real estate companies and product manufacturers benefit greatly from QR codes, but more and more businesses are deploying them.

The importance of deepening and enriching your customers' experience cannot be overestimated. Think of Pareto's Principle, the so-called "80/20 rule" that has become vogue in marketing strategy: 80 percent of your business will come from 20 percent of your customers. While connecting the outside world to your business, your mobile app should be especially dedicated to regular customers and clients. They will be the first to know about your app, and they will be the first to advertise it to others. You can ride high on the pecking order in an app store, get good search engine optimization, promote it through your location or website until your face turns blue, or advertise it in print or digital media, but your repeat customers will be your best promoters. If they feel enriched by their experience with you, they will see to it that others benefit from your business, too.

CLICKING IN: TAKEAWAY POINTS

- The mobile app is the best technological tool for upselling ever developed. It keeps your customer directly in touch with you every day. Never has your customer or client been so close to you on a 24/7 basis.
- Upselling keeps your doors open. Twenty percent of your customers buy 80 percent of your products and services. Use your app to continually deliver options for the loyal customer to do more business with you.
- All traditional retail and business-to-business upselling strategies can be adapted to the mobile app.
- When you develop upselling strategies that are specifically delivered through your mobile app, you create a major advantage over your competitors who are not connected to their customers through mobile devices.

CHAPTER TEN
MOVING FORWARD WITH AN APP THAT ROCKS

We have embarked on a wonderful journey. We have shown how more and more businesses understand, appreciate and operate within the mobile world. We have discussed the fundamental shift in the way business is conducted today, including customer perceptions of their own clout (once powerless, now extensive), and the prevalence of technology in determining how people will buy and sell products and services. We have determined the necessity of building a mobile app for your business, and shown how it connects you with customers and strengthens loyalty through its instantaneous communications, social networking, shopping, informational, and promotional features.

Now, it's time to look ahead. According to Jeanniey Mullen, there really is no other way to view the future if you want to remain relevant and continue to build your customer base.

"This is short and sweet. My personal view is that smartphones will become our wallets within the next two years," Mullen says. "And, apps will become the secure walls that keep our information. Mobile network operators will make a play to own a percentage of every transaction made with a smartphone, in order to grow by leaps and bounds and support the economy."

Where do you, the small business, fit into this world of smartphones, apps and mobile networks? In the middle, hopefully. Which means that NOW is the time to build a mobile app, if you haven't already done so. We have highlighted numerous features that mobile apps provide, as well as specific strategies to use in conjunction with your app to increase your sales and retain customers for the long haul. Obviously, if you own a longstanding business such as a medical practice, law firm or clothing store, these strategies are best practiced in person. However, even for these business categories, it makes smart sense to invest a little money and deploy a mobile app that increases your marketing reach and connects with your customers in their communications hubs: smartphones and/or tablets.

As you move forward, and work with your app development consultant, what should you look for? "Deciding what your customer wants in an app is often a tough area to be successful in," Mullen says. "It requires as much strategy as it does foresight. And, no matter what you decide, you will find yourself needing to adjust on the fly and revise your best efforts. The app space is still very new, and your app is being built, in part, on functionality defined by customers. It's also being built in part on functionalities that haven't ever existed before."

In other words, when you make the decision to build an app, come into the development process with an eye on "The Seven Must-Haves":

- Purpose
- Platform
- Price
- Presence
- Promise
- Functionality
- Flexibility

Let's tour the first five must-haves, and the competitive advantages they can bring you. Zinio's Mullen offers her insight on each point:

1. Purpose: "What is the main purpose of the app? Is it to drive an action, like a purchase; to drive intent, like engagement with a brand; or to drive excitement, like a game you want to share with your friends? All three purposes require very different app designs."
2. Platform: "What platforms will your app run on? iOS, Android, Windows, Mac, PC? Will your app be generic enough to run across all devices easily, or will you customize it to the device manufacturer to create an enhanced experience?"
3. Price: "Will your app be free (to the customer or client), or have a price? And, what offers will you have inside the app for payment, if any? This is a key differentiator, in many cases."
4. Presence: "Will the app present your brand (or store, products or services) successfully to the consumer who has never heard of you? Or does it require some sort of brand relationship? The ease of use of your app will speak volumes. Customer surveys can be very helpful here."
5. Promise: "Will your app live up to future innovations? Do you need to design a virtual world in your app? Or is a Twitter feed enough? Is your app flexible enough to integrate Google maps into it (so users can easily get directions to your location)?"

Now, for a glimpse into the final two Must-Haves:

6. FUNCTIONALITY: There is no point building an app if it is not functional. That's a lesson businesses learned the hard way in the late 1990s and early 2000s, when they created fancy websites loaded with sexy bells and whistles — only to fall flat when people sought ease of use and quicker navigation. Determine what your goals are, and how you want the app to function. Ease of use means everything in a mobile app.

7. FLEXIBILITY: Flexibility in design is essential. As Mullen pointed out earlier, mobile app technology is evolving rapidly, and more and more features are becoming available. Apps are easy for developers to modify and upgrade. Keep your app flexible, keep it very user-friendly to people who want it now, and know that you can meet their growing use requirements with some very simple upgrades.

Adapt your mobile strategy to a changing business climate. Welcome employee and customer input. They are the front liners, so they will know what is working at any given moment. The idea you have for the app today might become outdated in six months. By putting in a flexible, basic infrastructure, you make it possible to add subsequent features — or entire apps — to that infrastructure in a way that gives you more and more mobile clout. These days, it is essential strategy.

As a business, you have four choices when choosing to build an app:

1. DO NOTHING. We've already established this choice as an ill-advised path when more and more people are going mobile.

2. GET AN APP BUILT WITH ENTIRELY CUSTOMIZED FEATURES. It is difficult to find and communicate with a reputable app builder, because they tend to be more concerned with the technological marvels of their app design than the functional services you and your business need. Once they turn over the app and you pay the invoice, that's it. There is little to no follow up.

3. FIND A PLATFORM TO BUILD IT YOURSELF. This is cheaper than the second option, for sure. It begins by googling "mobile business apps." Then it's up to you. A certain challenge to consider: Can you afford to spend hundreds of hours (or more) going through the steep learning curve to work with tools and technologies you may never have seen before? You would need to learn a complex graphics program such as Photoshop, plus other programs, if you want the app to function well. Unless you know an app developer who can stand by your side, your outcome will not be optimal.

4. THE HYBRID OPTION. This is your best approach. By far. You can combine a mass production platform of features that keeps your costs down, with an app service provider that takes care of all the sticking points *and* works with you to fine-tune the app to your business needs. This service provider will solve glitches, consult with you regularly on your app's performance, change and upgrade when needed, and keep your business and customers first and foremost in mind. Instead of fighting with the app, you'll be enjoying the added business that comes from it.

Most small businesses only need an app that will serve their customers in a useful, interactive manner. That means sticking to the basics. For example, a local realtor might not need an app that plays videos of each home she lists, but quality photos and home listing descriptions would be perfect. As well as contact information.

Now for the big question: What does all of this cost? Who will build your app to best suit your business? To whom can you turn whenever your business or customer base shifts, and you need to adjust, upgrade or modify your app to match increased growth and demand?

The answer varies. In a sense, it's like buying a car. What kind of car? A luxury sedan? A sports utility vehicle? A compact? What is the cost range? Is a mobile app even feasible with your marketing budget?
The short answer? YES, especially with the development tools already available. Your app development consultant can focus on your specific business needs, and consult with you on how to design your app to meet them directly. This was not the case even two years (or, to put it another way, 15 billion app downloads) ago, when app technology was being developed and refined on the fly — and much of the cost was assed to early adopters. Some people spent tens or hundreds of thousands of dollars. Some still do.

However, we are in a new place now. Phase one is finished. The $2,000 flat screen TV of 2007 has become the $250 flat screen of today — bigger, clearer, more powerful, and infinitely less expensive. The same applies to apps. Millions of generic and customized apps are available; thousands more are being created daily, and development tools are growing. You could not have asked for a better time to build your app and put it on the market — especially since use is expected to skyrocket through the decade.

Quality app service providers are just that. They work *with* your business and your objectives to figure out exactly what you need, rather than to build an app and say, "Here ... take it or leave it." With full service consultation, the app development consultant finds out your specific needs, and collaborates with you on the app design. Next, your development consultant builds the app, counsels and advises you through the process so that you understand every aspect and potential use, and then works with you to get maximum value. This works just as well with business-to-business apps as with business-to-consumer versions.

How wonderful is that?

Take the step that is resulting in greater sales and customer bases for more and more forward-thinking businesses. Join the App Nation, utilize a mobile app, and enjoy the steady returns.

CLICKING IN: TAKEAWAY POINTS

- Now is the time to build a mobile app, if you haven't made that decision already. According to one expert, smartphones will become as essential as our wallets by 2014 — and apps will be the central connection to our shopping, event, informational, navigation and social networking needs.
- Develop your app with an eye on the seven "must-haves": purpose, platform, price, presence, promise, functionality and flexibility.
- Work with an app development platform service and with a apps building expert to receive the combination of features, consultation, ongoing service and pricing to assure that your customers receive the greatest possible experience with your business through your app.
- Get started. Make contact to build your app now. Migrate to the place where more and more of your customers are heading.

INDEX OF
ILLUSTRATIONS
AND TABLES

STATISTICAL
RESOURCES

In compiling this book, we derived statistical information and comparisons from numerous public surveys and reports. We cited the sources directly in the book. These surveys and reports were released by the following organizations, all of whom we thank:

- ABI Research
- Appstore
- CMO Council
- Compuware
- Comscore
- DC Financial Insights
- Deloitte
- eDigital Research
- eMarketer
- Kleiner Perkins Caulfield Byers (KPCB)
- Luxury Institute
- Mercator Advisory Group
- Microsoft Tag
- Mobile Advertising Survey
- Nielsen
- Nielsen McKinsey Incite (NM Incite)
- Pew Internet Report
- Portaltech Reply
- Prosper Mobile Insights
- Research By In-Stat
- Leo J. Shapiro and Associates
- Telemetrics
- The eTailing Group
- Wave Collapse
- xAd
- Zinio.com

EPILOGUE

You may be wondering why a cutting edge book on mobile apps doesn't have its own app.

Good question!

Well, the answer is a bit embarrassing...but only a bit. We thought long and hard about what app feature would bring more value to the reader. And we didn't come up with any great ideas.

Sure, we could make the book accessible from the app. But reader apps already do that very effectively. And all of the other ideas we had were kind of like that...maybe cute but not really representing a great improvement on the user experience.

Our belief is that mobile apps are a fantastic and unique tool, unlike any other. We don't want to poorly represent that belief by putting something out there that brings yawns. We want to eat our own food and we don't want it to be bland and boring.

So, please accept this as your invitation to help us out.

If you have a great new idea(s) on how to integrate the book experience with the mobile app experience, please let us know...as fast as you possibly can.

By the way, the best idea that we use will be rewarded with a brand spanking new Apple iPad Mini.

And, what's more, we'll appreciate your contribution very much.

You can submit your idea on our website at www.appnationbook.com.

And if you have any other thoughts, ideas, comments or questions, please visit our Facebook page at www.facebook.com/appnation1, or email us at info@sunstonepublishing.com.

Finally, welcome to App Nation! We've been waiting for you.

www.ingramcontent.com/pod-product-compliance
Lightning Source LLC
Chambersburg PA
CBHW041144050326
40689CB00001B/470